THE
COMPLETE
BOOK OF
MACAWS

THE COMPLETE BOOK OF MACAWS

ROSEMARY LOW

American Consulting Editor
Matthew M. Vriends PhD

BARRON'S

First edition for the United States published 1990 by Barron's
Educational Series, Inc
Published 1990 by Merehurst Limited, UK.

© Copyright 1990 Merehurst Limited

All inquiries should be addressed to:
Barron's Educational Series, Inc.
250 Wireless Boulevard
Hauppauge, New York 11788

International Standard Book No. 0–8120–6073–3
International Standard Book No. 0–8120–9037–3
Library of Congress Card No. 90–37666

Library of Congress Cataloguing-in-Publication Data
Low. Rosemary
    The complete book of macaws/Rosemary Low; consulting editor
Matthew M. Vriends. –– 1st ed. for the U.S.

    Includes bibliographical references and index.
    ISBN 0–8120–6073–3
    1. Macaws.   I. Vriends, Matthew M., 1937–   II. Title.
    SF473.M33L69   1990
    636.6′865––dc20   90–37666
                                                                          CIP

To MIKE

AUTHOR'S NOTE

In this book I have attempted to provide as much information as possible
which is relevant to macaws and to omit that which applies to parrots in
general. Therefore, in the chapter which discusses disease and the care of
sick birds, for example, I have not included information on how to recognize
an ailing bird, but instead have given details of some of the more recently
recognized virus diseases, such as papova, to which macaws are susceptible.

I have also presented as much new data on breeding as possible (much of it
from the birds in my care) so that there is little or no overlap with the text of
Parrots, their Care and Breeding (1986).

I would like to thank Wolfgang Kiessling, my former employer at Loro
Parque, Tenerife and my present employers, Klaus Paulmann and Carlos
Bottcher, at Palmitos Park, Gran Canaria for the opportunity to work with
this very rewarding and intelligent group of parrots. They capture the heart
like no other birds!

Editor: Lesley Young
Designer: Carole Perks
Typesetting by Deltatype Ltd, Ellesmere Port, UK
Reprographics by J Film Process Ltd, Bangkok, Thailand
Printed in Portugal by Printer Portuguesa Industria Grafica LDA

Contents

1
What is a Macaw?

Large macaws comprise one of the few groups of tropical birds that are easily recognizable. Along with a few others, such as cockatoos and toucans, they are sufficiently distinct and popular to be readily distinguishable. Asked to describe a macaw, the average person would probably reply that it is a large, gaudily colored parrot with a long tail.

In fact, this description accurately defines only 11 of the 17 species. All have long tails and are gaudy – but bearing in mind that parrots are known for their brilliant colors, six of the small macaws are not especially colorful. The same six are not large either, measuring 50 cm (19 in.) or under. Most people would not recognize the three smallest species as macaws.

rule! They are also very distinctive birds which are obviously macaws.

There are two macaw-like parrots which are not classified as macaws. They are the Thick-billed Parrot (*Rhynchopsitta pachyrhyncha*), which would probably be classified as a macaw if it had a longer tail, and the Yellow-eared Conure or Parrot (*Ognorhynchus icterotis*). If its lores were bare it, too, would surely be called a macaw! It has bare skin surrounding the lower mandible and the macaw-like habit of blushing when excited. It can thus be seen that, as a group, the macaws are by no means as well defined as at first might be thought.

If I define a macaw as a parrot with a tail of the same length as its body or longer, and with the lores bare or the skin surrounding the lower mandible bare, all known species are included and macaw-like parrots, such as *Ognorhynchus*, are excluded. This seems to be a rather fragile combination of characteristics! Perhaps comparative cytogenetics will provide the true answer. As yet, this science, which can be used to interpret the evolutionary relationships of different groups of animals, is in its infancy where parrots are concerned.

Macaws possess no other characteristics to set them apart from other neotropical parrots, which form a homogeneous group (of the same kind). In contrast, the parrots of Australia, for example, belong to widely differing and totally unrelated genera. Basically, the large macaws differ from other neotropical parrots mainly in their sheer size; thus their feet are enormous and their tongues are the largest and fleshiest of any parrots'. The difference between the smallest macaw, the Hahn's, and some of the *Aratinga* conures

Unlike the other large *Ara* macaws, the Scarlet Macaw does not have small lines of feathers decorating the cheeks

These are the Yellow-collared, Illiger's and Hahn's. They could easily mistake them for conures, which are parakeets from South and Central America. The principal difference is that these macaws have the lores (the area between beak and eye) devoid of feathers. However, this is not a feature that can be used to define a macaw, as the *Anodorhynchus* species have feathered lores. They are the exception which defies the

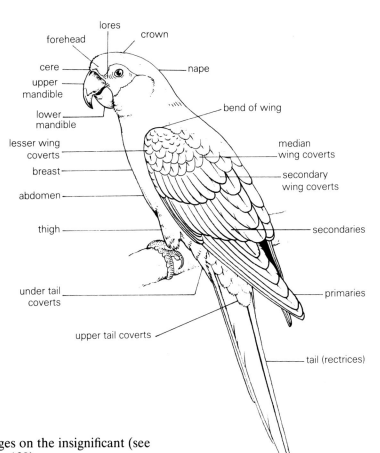

lores
forehead
crown
cere
nape
upper mandible
lower mandible
bend of wing
lesser wing coverts
median wing coverts
breast
secondary wing coverts
abdomen
thigh
secondaries
under tail coverts
primaries
upper tail coverts
tail (rectrices)

verges on the insignificant (see page 139).

One of the reasons why macaws, Amazons, conures and some other neotropical parrots are so loved as companion birds is their affectionate nature. Many Australian parrots are just as brightly colored but, with the exception of the cockatoos, they seldom show affection towards people. The explanation is linked to their lifestyle. The Australian parrots (except the cockatoos) do not form strong pair bonds. Many are nomadic, most are found in flocks and the members of the flock pair off only during the breeding season. In contrast, most neotropical parrots (those from South and Central America) form very strong pair bonds, and even if the birds are members of a flock, male and female keep together within the flock. They show great affection and devotion to their mate and offspring.

In captivity, a tame bird transfers this affection to its closest human friend if kept alone as a pet. Indeed, the love and devotion that a large macaw can show to its owner is quite extraordinary. One has to experience this to realize how strong the bond can be. It is easy to understand how, for a childless person, for example, a macaw can become almost a child substitute. Macaws can be quite extraordinarily gentle, affectionate and trustworthy. Alas, not all have such appealing natures, however. Indeed, comparatively few are totally trustworthy, and no one should attempt to touch a macaw he or she does not know.

From Mexico to Argentina

Macaws are found only in the neotropical region, i.e., throughout the tropical areas of South and Central America and Mexico. They range as far north as northern Mexico (southeastern Sonora and southwestern Chihuahua), where the Military Macaw occurs, as far south as northeastern Argentina, where Illiger's is found in Misiones, and northern Paraguay and northwestern Argentina (Juyuy and Salta), where the Yellow-collared occurs. The distribution areas of wide-ranging species have diminished greatly in the past three or four decades and, regrettably, will continue to decline until some species are brought close to extinction, perhaps surviving only in national parks or other "protected" areas.

One extinction
One macaw is known to have become extinct since about 1885. This is the Cuban (see page 124). Eight other extinct macaws have also been named. A subfossil tibiotarsus is regarded as evidence of the existence of the Saint Croix Macaw (*Ara autocthones*) from Saint Croix in the Virgin Islands. For the other extinct species there is no tangible evidence, however, and, except in the case of the Yellow-headed Macaw (*Ara gossei*) from Jamaica, reports of the existence of other species are not very convincing, although there could well have been other macaws on the Caribbean islands. When habitats are disturbed, macaws are the first parrots to become extinct. While the Cuban Amazon (*Amazona l. leucocephala*) and the Cuban Conure (*Aratinga euops*) survive, the Cuban Macaw became extinct over a century ago.

Today, if one includes the Glaucous Macaw, 17 species of macaws survive.

Classification of macaws
The macaws are arranged in three or four genera. The large, best-known members of the group are classified as *Ara*, as are those known as dwarf macaws, with the exception of Hahn's and Noble macaws, which are placed in the genus *Diopsittaca* by some taxonomists. The three striking blue macaws of the genus *Anodorhynchus*, of which the Hyacinthine is the best known, are unmistakable and might even be considered conspecific. Finally, there is Spix's, placed in the monotypic (containing only one species) genus *Cyanopsitta*. It is the most distinctive of all macaws.

Of the 17 species, 13 are well known, or fairly well known, in aviculture, two (Lear's and Spix's) exist but are extremely rare, and two (Coulon's and Glaucous) are unknown. (Rumors do exist of Coulon's in the United States.) It can thus be seen that, as a group, the macaws are well represented in captivity. A great deal more should be known about them than is actually the case; however, it is only since the mid-1970s that there has been a high degree of interest in breeding these birds.

Macaws as pets
Previously, probably 95 percent were kept as pets without companions of their own species. Macaws are not only highly social but also highly intelligent; thus keeping them on their own is a form of emotional torture unless they are "bonded" to their owner, that is, regard him or her as a mate. Unfortunately, it is still considered fashionable today to keep a single macaw as a pet. Many people who do so cherish their macaw as a member of the family and indulge its every whim. Other macaws are treated with a total lack of understanding, respect or compassion.

The Blue and Yellow Macaw, *Ara ararauna*, is the most widely kept of the large macaws

In suitable surroundings some large macaws can be allowed to fly at liberty for a period each day

In this book it will be emphasized that *large* macaws are not considered suitable as house pets. Now that all species are threatened and endangered by loss of habitat and excessive trading, it would not be ethical to promote them as pets. Only the Blue and Yellow Macaw is being reared in sufficient numbers in captivity for this maxim not to apply. Even so, I hesitate to recommend that it be kept as a pet because relatively few people have the time or the temperament necessary to keep a large macaw content.

Macaws are exceptional parrots. Having kept parrots for over 30 years, since my teenage days, and bred them for 27 years or so, I have been fortunate enough to have worked with almost all of the species of parrots available in aviculture, including approximately 215 species at Loro Parque, Tenerife, during the time I spent there as curator. All the macaws were included in this collection, except Glaucous, Lear's and Coulon's. All except Spix's, Severe and Yellow-collared were represented by several pairs. It was fascinating to study the behavior and personalities of different species and of members of the same species, and to compare macaws with other parrots. It can be misleading to speak of intelligence because often what we describe in this way is an adaptation to captivity based on some aspect of a species' natural behavior. Generally speaking, however, the larger parrots are more intelligent than the smaller ones, and macaws, cockatoos and some Amazons would appear to be the most intelligent of all. To me, the appeal of macaws has less to do with their spectacular colors and more to do with their individual personalities. Don't underestimate them. Expect them all to be as different as are your human friends and you will be on the right track to understanding them.

2
Conservation

All of the large species of macaws have declined over all or much of their range during this century. The decline for some species is very serious. No one will ever know the true extent of the reduction of their numbers because large macaws are very difficult to study in the wild and many of the areas they inhabit remain virtually unexplored as regards their fauna until they are actually being destroyed. Macaws are primarily rain-forest birds – and there can be no one who is unaware of the extent of the destruction of the rain forests in forests in South America, particularly in Brazil.

Every year we read new and horrifying statistics regarding deforestation. In Amazonia (Brazil's north region), for example, the deforested area increased from 125,000 sq km (48,260 sq mi) in 1980 to 600,000 sq km (231,660 sq mi) in 1988 (World Bank figures). In 1989 an area the size of West Germany – 248,651 sq km (96,000 sq mi) – will have been destroyed, unless some means can be found of stopping the destruction, which seems highly unlikely.

Everyone knows that it is in people's own interests to preserve the rain forests and that the world will become a desert without them. Brazil contains 30 percent of the earth's surviving rain forests, in an area that could contain much of the United States, stretching from California to New York. As shown by the "green revolution" which began to gather momentum in the late 1980s, most ordinary people are concerned about such plundering of the earth's reserves but feel powerless to do anything about it. However, power does not lie solely in the hands of governments, for, ultimately, politicians must listen to the voices of the ordinary people. Perhaps in Brazil such people will never be wealthy enough to concern themselves with ecological matters – except those that affect their next meal – but beyond those countries which have within their boundaries the richest of all earth's natural habitats – the rain forest – are millions of consumers of products of those rain forests. These are not just the infamous beefburger (most of Brazil's beef is exported and ranching was said to account for 72 percent of the areas which had been cleared by 1989). Other products of the forests, not the least important of which are parrots, also earn large revenues.

Worldwide, no family of tropical birds has a larger trade in wild-caught specimens than parrots, popular in many households for their ability to mimic, their brilliant colors, their

The range of macaws in the wild

affectionate ways and clever behavior. At the time of writing, the majority of those offered in pet shops have been captured in the wild. But is the average person who buys such a bird aware of this? Would he or she still purchase it if the high mortality rate involved in this trade was made known?

For nearly 20 years, since the early 1970s, parrots – especially macaws – have been traded in unacceptably high numbers. Many of these were young birds taken from the nest in their native habitat and fed by people with no proper knowledge of nutrition or hygiene, and without the ability to save those that inevitably became ill. It would be optimistic to say that, on average, one in ten survived to reach a foreign country, and many that did died soon afterwards.

Declining trade

Although this trade continues, the writing is on the wall and there is every indication that it will not survive, except on a small scale, for very much longer. The state of New York has already made the sale of wild-caught tropical birds illegal (the sale of native birds has long been banned). In the 1980s many South American countries prohibited the export of their native fauna. CITES is the convention which regulates the Trade in Endangered Species of Wild Fauna and Flora, also known as the Washington Convention. This came into effect in 1975 and established rules for commercial and noncommercial trade. Over 100 countries are now signatories and comply with CITES rules.

The species covered by CITES are listed in three appendices. Those on Appendix I are endangered and trade is permitted only in exceptional circumstances. Unfortunately, this does not mean that trade has ceased altogether; it can still occur in countries which are not signatories to CITES, while the smuggling of birds of desirable species also occurs, regardless of legislation. Macaws on Appendix I are Hyacinthine, Lear's, Glaucous, Blue-throated (Caninde), Scarlet, Military, Buffon's, Red-fronted and Spix's.

Appendix II lists species which could become endangered unless their trade is regulated. In fact, the list is contentious because all parrots not on Appendix I are on Appendix II, except the Budgerigar and the Cockatiel. They are on Appendix III and may be regarded as in no danger. Thus all the other species of macaw appear on Appendix II and their commercial trade is permitted.

It is no wonder that the large species of macaws have fared so badly in the wild. Large parrots – but especially large macaws – are the first species to disappear when habitats are disturbed. This occurs partly because their numbers have already been reduced by trapping, partly because they have much slower reproduction rates than the smaller parrots, and partly because, when forests are selectively logged and the large trees removed, the number of nesting sites which remain for large parrots declines seriously. This number is reduced again, perhaps to a catastrophic degree, because of the practice of many trappers of cutting down nest trees to obtain young. These may be new settlers who know nothing of nature. They are often very poor and seize the opportunity to make some money today with no thought for tomorrow.

Pressures on wild populations

Populations of parrots can tolerate trade at a reasonable level for some years, or even indefinitely in an undisturbed habitat. Most can also tolerate some habitat disturbance, but they are unable to cope with these combined pressures. Since the early 1970s, some of the large macaws, such as the Hyacinthine, the Scarlet and the Green-winged, have completely disappeared from large parts of their ranges. For example, the Green-winged and the Blue and Yellow are now extinct in southeastern Brazil. When I was there in 1988 I visited the Iguaçu Falls. There, a massive hydroelectric plant spans the river

The range of the Green-winged Macaw has declined significantly. It is already extinct in Argentina and southeast Brazil

between Argentina and Brazil. Only 20 years previously Green-winged Macaws had been nesting in this river bank. A week previously I had been staying on a farm situated two hours' drive from São Paulo at Pirassununga. The last Green-winged Macaw was seen here in 1935 – also the last Hyacinthine. In Argentina, the Green-winged is believed to have become extinct in 1917.

Field studies on macaws pose great difficulties and few have been carried out. Knowledge of the basic facts of their natural history has only recently been acquired. Since 1985, Charles Munn, an energetic American ornithologist, has been studying three large species of *Ara* in southeastern Peru: the Blue and Yellow, Scarlet and Green-winged. Of the eight nests found up to 1986, five failed and only five young were fledged from the other three nests. The study area was in a national park of extensive forest, with no disturbance and no hunting – apparently optimum conditions. Munn (1988b) described the birds' reproductive rate as "glacially slow". He believes that some young stay with their parents for more than one year. This could mean that the species does not breed every year. If this slow reproduction rate is true of the large macaws generally, it is not

difficult to imagine the impact that the collection of thousands of nestlings per annum has had on the populations.

Munn wrote of his data from the 1986–8 nesting seasons:

We had to search hard to find active nests, and of the adult macaws more than 80 percent had no offspring flying with them at the end of the nesting season in April. (The season begins in November.) Of the 20 nests of blue-and-yellow, scarlet, and red-and-green [*chloroptera*] macaws that we observed, seven failed, and most of the individually recognizable, fully mature blue-and-yellow macaws that appeared daily in the section of the river near these active nests had neither of the two physical features indicative of breeders: huge, food-filled crops, or throat pouches (especially on males), and tattered, lackluster body and tail features. . . . I would estimate that 100 pairs of large macaws might fledge as few as 15–25 young per year. Such a low reproductive rate indicates that macaws *cannot* be harvested from the wild without depleting their populations.

Why is the reproduction rate so low? Charles Munn's study, which commenced in 1984, is providing

12

the first systematic data on the biology of seven macaw species in Manu. There is a great deal to learn. Systematic studies on macaws elsewhere are virtually nonexistent. In northern Peru there is less disturbance and less hunting than in any other area of the Amazon, and thus the reproduction rate should be better here than elsewhere. Why is it so low? Munn thought that one reason could be a shortage of nest sites. Dead palms are the favorite sites of Blue and Yellow and of Green-winged Macaws, but apparently most dead palms fall during the following year and Munn knew of only one example of a nest being used during the next season.

He also recorded what must surely be aberrant behavior, perhaps due to the lack of nests. One nest failed after it was entered by other macaws when the parents were absent; in another case a young Blue and Yellow Macaw was killed by other macaws which entered its nest. This would make sense only if the birds visiting the nest wanted to take it over for themselves.

Usually field studies on parrots are not carried out until a species is endangered. Several such studies—(for example, the Thick-billed Parrot, *Rhynchopsitta pachyrhyncha*, in Mexico and the Puerto Rican Parrot, *Amazona vittata* (Low, 1984)—have highlighted a lack of nesting sites, or of suitable nesting sites, as a major cause of low reproduction rates.

It is, of course, difficult to find the nests of large macaws, which may be as high as 20–30 m (66–100 ft) above the ground, and equally difficult to investigate them, as one cannot climb a dead palm. It is necessary to hang from an adjoining tree, wearing a climbing harness. Studying the breeding biology of macaws is therefore extremely awkward and great credit must go to those involved.

Charles Munn wrote:

With data still so scarce, we remain largely ignorant of how to preserve healthy wild populations of macaws. But save these populations we must. Their sublime beauty, intelligence, and fascinating behavior are enough justification to pursue their preservation. Beyond this we may have much to gain from the systematic study of macaws. Discovering their mechanism for detoxifying natural poisons, learning how they apparently remember the location of food sources in hundreds of square miles of rain forests, and cataloguing their elaborate vocal repertoire could lead to important discoveries in biochemistry as well as in the biology of communication, memory and intelligence.

The most obvious step to take in the preservation of these magnificent denizens of the rain forest is to make their capture illegal in all the countries in which they occur. This would not be easy to implement. Although most countries where macaws occur no longer permit their export, the domestic trade is quite large. Macaws are shot for food and for their plumage, the young are taken for pets, and young and adults are taken for the illegal trade, to be smuggled out of the country.

Many countries have not ratified CITES and can therefore legally import endangered species. As a result Appendix I species, such as large macaws, are still being captured for trade – but thankfully in smaller numbers as since the mid 1980s most of the South American countries ceased to export their fauna.

Demand for macaw feathers
The local demand for macaws must not be forgotten. Regrettably, a large trade in the highly decorative tail feathers of macaws, especially Scarlet and Military, has existed for hundreds of years. The feathers have been used in the ceremonial costumes of Indians in the southwestern states of the United States since at least AD 1100, it is

A group of wild
Red-bellied
Macaws visiting a
source of water

believed. According to Schneider (1985–6), the birds were maintained alive

. . . under intolerable conditions in rooms with little light; and periodically stripped of their feathers for ceremonial use. They lived as long as their systems could tolerate the conditions. They died and more were traded for. Upon examination of sample skeletal remains, many of which were buried or found in trash mounds, indications of premature old age were displayed; a metabolic deficit contributed to by lack of sunshine and proper food. Of the 145 skeletal remains studied, the greater number of specimens were assigned to the age of slightly over one year at the time of death.

Schneider quotes the sad case of a Military Macaw given to a Zuni Indian in 1924. "This bird, denuded of feathers at intervals, died in 1946. This Macaw struggled to live for 22 years under inhumane and deplorable conditions as a producer of feathers for Indian rituals."

Apparently, Aztec dance groups from Mexico, which tour the United States, have headdresses containing dozens of macaw tail feathers. They sell some of these as they tour. In Peru every year, during the Snow Star Pilgrimage, hundreds of participants wear feathered costumes and carry staffs to which are affixed macaw tail feathers.

Local trade in macaws for feathers probably occurs in most countries of South and Central America and also in Panama. There, rural people use the tail feathers in their traditional dances, some of which are staged as tourist attractions. According to Schneider, the feathers are used in the dancers' headdresses, each of which contains 60 to 80 tail feathers, preferably from Scarlet Macaws. In 1983, tail sets (the middle five to seven feathers) from nearly 150 Military Macaws were brought into the United States from Mexico, in one shipment, and sold in Arizona, to Indians.

In Panama, the capture of macaws for feathers has a long tradition. However, in recent years it has become a serious problem. The feathers are used in the headdresses of costumes worn for local folk dances. The increasing popularity of the folk dance has led to the formation of dance groups throughout the country. All the dancers seek macaw feathers for their costumes. ICBP-Panama (International Council for Bird Preservation), in collaboration with aviculturists and institutions outside Panama, therefore initiated a project to collect macaw feathers. The feathers are hired out for a modest fee. However, many more wing and tail feathers are needed. This provides a chance for private aviculturists to assist in the conservation of the birds they so admire. Those who wish to donate tail and wing feathers (which must be in good condition) should first write to Francisco D. Delgado, CIPA-ICBP, Seccion Nacional Panama, Apartado 278, Chitre-Herrera, Panama.

The World Parrot Trust

In 1989, the formation of the World Parrot Trust was announced. This should prove to be an important step forward in the conservation of macaws and other parrots. The Trust's introductory literature states:

. . . we must combine our forces to work for the survival and welfare of the parrots.

We know, of course, that much is being done. International conferences are held, research is under way, some effective field projects are in place. CITES has made a valuable contribution. ICBP have appointed a Parrot Officer to concentrate efforts to save the parrots, and many governments worldwide are doing their best to help the situation.

We believe that the missing element is popular, organised and universal support for the conservation of parrots. In time, The World Parrot Trust can provide a meeting point for all organisations and all people of goodwill who wish to see habitats preserved, species protected, captive breeding programmes developed, and reintroductions being achieved. In addition, the Trust intends to work for the welfare of the countless individual parrots which are currently being kept as pets in inadequate conditions. . . .

The Trust believes that enlightened aviculture *is* conservation. It invites everyone who keeps and cares about parrots to join as soon as possible, and start the work which is urgently needed to save many parrot species from extinction.

Further information can be obtained from: The World Parrot Trust, c/o Paradise Park, Hayle, Cornwall, United Kingdom TR27 4HY, telephone: 0736 753365.

The key to conservation

Preservation of their habitat is, of course, the key to the conservation of wild macaws. The decade of the 1980s was the one in which conservation of the world's rain forests became a global issue – but, alas, most of the enthusiasm and interest was among those outside the tropics. Persuading nations such as Brazil to act before it is too late will be a very different matter. By the time this occurs, some species of macaws will already be extinct in the wild. It is fortunate, indeed, that macaws nest so readily in captivity. They will at least survive here for future generations to admire their extravagant colors, magnificent form and appealing personalities. However, a macaw without a forest (or its other natural habitat) is not a real macaw. You must see these imposing birds in flight above the forest canopy, or their massed colors when dozens congregate to collect minerals or clay, or hear their shrieks and raucous cries harmonize with their surroundings, to know the real macaw. This privilege will be accorded to fewer and fewer people unless some means can be found to halt the greatest human folly to date – the destruction of the rain forests.

3
Buying a Macaw

What a trap for the unwary buying a macaw is! If you have kept and bred birds for many years, you know the pitfalls of buying – but all too often macaws attract people who know nothing at all about birds. Such innocents are likely to be the victims of unscrupulous sellers, to end up with plucked birds ("molting"), biters or screamers, or other unfortunate macaws whose neglect has resulted in emotional problems. If you want to buy a macaw for a pet, go to a breeder and obtain a hand-fed youngster. It will be adorably tame, has known no other owner, is indisputably young and will not be suffering from any of the diseases which make imported birds such a risk. Naturally, bearing in mind all these advantages, you can expect to pay considerably more for a domestically bred bird.

These remarks are directed at the potential owner of a pet macaw, as parrot breeders will be familiar with the avicultural magazines most likely to carry advertisements for captive-bred macaws. Most people attracted to the idea of keeping a macaw in the home have no idea of what is involved. Their motives may be totally misguided: they believe it is trendy to keep a large, spectacular, exotic bird, or they want something gaudy to complement the décor. These ideas are unthinkable to those who understand what demanding and sensitive creatures the large macaws are.

I doubt whether one person in five hundred, possibly one in a thousand, has the necessary sympathetic attitude – and such a person may not have enough spare time. In short, the large macaws cannot be considered suitable house pets: their emotional requirements are difficult to meet; they are very noisy and extremely destructive. They are most certainly not suitable for the house-proud. Moreover, by no stretch of the imagination can a large macaw be considered a family pet. Its beak is a powerful weapon which can inflict very serious injury; its nails are very sharp and easily puncture the flesh unless regularly filed, and its sheer weight—in the region of 1 kg (2 lb)—and strength can make it difficult to handle.

On the other hand, the small or miniature macaws, that is, those smaller than and including the Severe Macaw, make enchanting pets. Their smaller size makes keeping them in a house or apartment much more practical; although demanding, they are less likely to suffer emotional problems which result in feather plucking or screaming.

Provided that great care is taken in closing all possible exits, dwarf or miniature macaws can be allowed supervised freedom within a room, and will gain great

Illiger's Macaw: Its inquisitive and alert personality is typical of the small macaws

enjoyment and healthy exercise from a period of freedom each day. It must be noted, however, that even they can be extremely destructive.

Most people do not have rooms of sufficient size for a large macaw to take to the wing; even if they did, the havoc caused by such excursions generally means that the macaw is soon confined to its cage – a cramped and boring existence. For those who insist on keeping large macaws as pets, I would suggest building an outdoor aviary where the macaw can exercise during the day, especially if the owner is at work. This is possible only if the difference between the indoor and the outdoor temperature is small.

Tame macaws are demanding!
A tame macaw is not like a dog, which will be content as long as it is around people and receives the occasional pat and word of endearment: it is a much more demanding creature. It needs to be let out of its cage and to monopolize your attention for at least half an hour each evening; to sit on your shoulder or even lie in your lap while you rub its head or tickle under its wings. It is not like a cockatoo, which will snuggle up to you and happily fall asleep while you watch television. If your attention wanders, a macaw may remind you of its presence with a little nip; that is, the nip may seem little to the macaw: it is not malicious but it does not lack strength!

If you want a large macaw because you believe it falls into the category of "talking parrot", think again. Very few learn more than a dozen words and, in any case, this motive is the greatest insult imaginable to a macaw's intelligence. Never underestimate the intelligence of the large macaws as, sadly, many people do. They are incapable of putting themselves in the macaw's place and realizing what a monotonous and unfulfilled life the unfortunate bird leads. While this is true also of most pet birds that have not formed a close

bond with their owners, few other species have the mental capacity of a large macaw, for which close and single confinement is the worst kind of imprisonment.

On the other hand, single dwarf macaws which have been obtained young make wonderful pets and often become talented talkers with bigger vocabularies than the large macaws. They are delightfully playful and inquisitive.

Most of the *large* macaws are now endangered, because of the combined pressures of trade and habitat destruction. This brings us to another point – is it ethical to keep endangered species as pets? In my opinion, it can be justified only if the intention is to breed when the birds are old enough. Let me pose another question, especially to readers in the United States. Is it ethical to breed macaw hybrids of which one of the parents is an endangered species such as a Scarlet? In the United States such hybrids are produced for the pet trade, sometimes utilizing birds which could have been used to produce pure-bred chicks of their own species.

Before making up your mind regarding the species of macaw to keep, visit a zoo or private collection which has a good range of species. Few zoos keep many of the dwarf macaws, however, so for these contact an avicultural society in your area and inquire about the names of macaw breeders. This may not prove easy but do not give up. Try also to obtain a cage-bird magazine. These magazines are published in all countries where aviculture is popular. Beware the classified advertisement column of your local newspaper as breeders seldom use such means of advertising. This might produce an inexpensive bird suitable for breeding and for keeping outdoors, but many macaws advertised thus are probably adults with vices and are not suitable as pets.

When you finally contact a breeder, remember that there are comparatively few specialist breeders of macaws and that most breeders have only two or three

Hyacinthine Macaws

Hyacinthine Macaw aged 64 days, hatched at Loro Parque, Tenerife

Hyacinthine Macaws will descend to the aviary floor to retrieve fallen items of food

The magnificent
Hyacinthine
Macaw, whose
numbers in the wild
have been
drastically reduced
by illegal trapping

pairs. Young will not be available all the year round.

Some aviculturists will allow you to visit their aviaries if you are a potential buyer. However, because of the high risk of theft, many breeders, especially the larger ones, do not.

Distinguishing captive-bred macaws
In the United States there are many excellent pet shops which sell domestically bred hand-raised macaws; this is rare in other countries. How will you know a genuine captive-bred bird from an imported youngster? The latter are seldom in good feather and almost invariably have the flight feathers cut on one or both wings, although a pet shop may do this if they display a macaw on a stand. However, a captive-bred bird should be in perfect feather; wild-caught young usually have some ragged feathers, or dark margins to many feathers. Some breeders put bands on their young birds; this is proof of captive-breeding.

How to tell the age of a macaw is a question which is often asked. The answer is that after a large macaw reaches about 18 months of age, or a dwarf macaw six months, there is no way of determining its age. Before then the eye color is significant. The eye color of adult macaws varies according to the species. In young birds it is an indistinct blackish gray, gradually becoming lighter over a period of many months in large *Ara* macaws, but attaining adult coloration as early as five months in small species.

Young macaws also have a partial molt, beginning with the head feathers, at five and a half to six months old.

I would strongly advise against buying a macaw as a pet without seeing it first. Even if the seller agrees to take the bird back if you do not like it, the stress which a change of owner causes to a macaw must be borne in mind.

Getting off to a good start
When you buy a macaw, realize that it needs to be treated with special sympathy at first. Do not let it be overwhelmed by the attention of every member of the family, who may have no understanding of its needs. Until it settles down, it is best handled and fed by only one or two people. It should be kept in the most lived-in room of the house, preferably at eye level or higher at first, so that it can get to know people without being prodded or teased. It should be spoken to (and petted, if tame) very often and offered tidbits three or four times a day.

It is advisable to have the bird checked by an avian veterinarian if there is one in your area. He or she will examine the bird and make routine tests such as fecal analysis. If you cannot find a veterinarian who is used to this kind of work, however, it would probably be a pointless exercise.

Start off as you mean to continue. Do not spend two hours a day with the bird on your hand if this routine cannot be maintained. When you devote less time to the bird, it will feel neglected and this may be the start of screaming sessions.

Most of all, remember that, with luck, your macaw will be in your care for many years to come. Because these birds are long-lived, make provision in your will for it to pass to a reliable individual or bird sanctuary.

Individual Green-winged Macaws can be recognized by the lines of feathers on the bare facial area, and by the extent of the black area on the upper mandible

4
Accommodation

There are still bird sanctuaries where macaws fly at liberty or, in the case of Loro Parque in Tenerife, where macaws are flown at liberty several times daily, returning to the trainer's hand on cue. Anyone intent on keeping macaws should try to see free-flying birds before starting to build an aviary. I suggest this because there is a trend (unacceptable to me) for keeping macaws in very small aviaries or suspended cages. It is impossible to appreciate the nature of a large macaw until one has seen it in flight. The need for larger cages should then be obvious.

Generally, macaws are adequately housed only in the better zoos or bird sanctuaries, partly because private owners may feel that they will lose contact with their birds in large aviaries and partly because such enclosures are extremely expensive to build. A compromise situation, which gives the best of both worlds, is provided by one aviculturist in England, Harry Sissen from Yorkshire. His idea deserves to be widely copied because it enables macaws to fly in a large area for much of the year, greatly improving breeding success through increased fertility. Outside of the breeding season, all the large macaws fly together in one aviary which measures 33 m (110 ft) long and 9 m (30 ft) wide.

Pairs which had been infertile for some years began to produce fertile eggs after this method was adopted. Some established pairs also changed partners. This was an important development because compatibility between male and female is a key factor in captive breeding success. Many long-term captive macaws fail to breed because they have been kept for years in cramped accommodation, their general condition is poor and they may also be overweight.

Regular flying exercise, coupled with a varied and healthy diet, is the best way to regain fitness and fertility.

A large flight area for macaws is more important than for many other parrots, some of which exercise by flying frequently between the perches at the front and back of even a small cage.

Macaws do not do this. Although their area may be large enough for flight, they will prefer to climb rather than fly. Place the same macaws in a much larger enclosure, however, and they will eventually fly instead of climbing.

I believe that the *height* is a very important dimension of an aviary for large macaws; after all, they are birds of the forest canopy and no doubt feel much more secure when they can look down on people. Large aviaries should be 3 m (10 ft) high.

Of course, most people are limited by space and finance and are unable to give every pair a large aviary, but they could either adopt Harry Sissen's idea of one very large communal aviary outside of the breeding season, or build suspended aviaries which are long and raised well off the ground, by

Wing-clipped macaws, such as these Blue and Yellows, can be given their freedom in an area surrounding their nest-box, but the locality must be entirely suitable. These macaws (at Loro Parque) have been clipped, but the last primary has been retained for the sake of appearance

Lear's and
Spix's Macaws

Lear's Macaw, an
extreme rarity in
captivity and in the
wild

Spix's Macaw at
Loro Parque,
Tenerife. This is
one of the rarest
birds in the world

One method of fixing perches is to fit them between two metal plates that are joined by screws

Covered service passages (such as these in the breeding center at Palmitos Park on Gran Canaria) have many advantages. Aviaries and nest-boxes (inspection doors on the right side of the passage) can be tended without fear of birds escaping. Cleaning and feeding can be carried out in comfort, regardless of weather conditions

at least 1.2 m (4 ft). Around the outside of Harry Sissen's aviary there are a number of small breeding aviaries, in which the birds are enclosed as they pair off.

Suspended cages
In recent years suspended cages have found favor with many breeders, especially in warmer climates, such as in the southern states of the United States. This design has a number of advantages. Discarded food and droppings fall through the bottom of the cage so the birds have no access to stale food or feces which may be harboring bacterial or fungal growth or, in the case of feces, parasites or their eggs. Vermin seldom enter because there is nowhere to hide. In addition, these cages are quick, easy and less expensive to construct than other types and can be readily moved.

The main disadvantage is that catching birds within a suspended cage is much more difficult. A minor disadvantage is that nuts, pieces of orange or other desirable food items may fall through the floor to the ground because macaws have the habit of removing items from the food tray rather than leaving them to be eaten later in the day.

These disadvantages can be overcome. A metal support at floor level can run the length of the cage and a door large enough for a person to enter can be made, allowing one to walk the length of the cage interior if necessary. Alternatively, the welded mesh on the roof can be cut along one section the width of the cage and a

framework of wood covered with welded mesh can be inserted to shut off a 1.8-m (6-ft) section of the cage. If all cages are of a standard width and height, it is necessary to construct only one such frame.

The suspended cage does not have to be rectangular in shape. At the Avicultural Institute, a large parrot-breeding center in California, which ceased to exist in 1987, two types of suspended cages were used for breeding the large macaws. The second was L-shaped and its purpose was to give extra privacy to some pairs. The dimensions were 3 m (10 ft) long, 91 cm (3 ft) wide and 1.2 m (4 ft) high, with an extension at the back, to form the L-shape, 1.2 m (4 ft) long and 91 cm (3 ft) wide. A horizontal nest barrel was mounted

Alternatively, cut the perch to the correct length so that it is a tight fit. The perch simply rests on a V-shaped piece of metal

24

outside the cage, the end with the entrance hole fitting against the extension and the end with the inspection door parallel to the front panel of the cage. The extension was surrounded with plywood to provide total privacy in the vicinity of the nest.

Dale Thompson (1986), former director of the Avicultural Institute, stated:

> The great advantage of the L-shaped cage is that the pair can completely avoid visual contact with the keeper, that is, they have some place to hide. They can retreat into the extension and defend the nest entrance, instead of jumping into the barrel. The result is less trauma to eggs and chicks.

This idea is highly recommended, especially for nervous birds.

My main objection to suspended cages is that breeders have a tendency to make them too small. Recommended sizes for large macaws are 4 m (13 ft) long, 2 m (6 ft 4 in) wide and 2 m high. There would be a problem with sagging if longer cages were constructed. If required, suspended cages are best built in the traditional aviary style. The suggested size of a cage for a small macaw, up to the size of a Severe, is 3 m (10 ft) long, 1 m (3 ft 4 in) wide and 3 m high. If 16-gauge welded mesh is used, the cage will bow outwards if it is longer than 3 m.

As already mentioned, large macaws feel more secure when they can look down on people and I therefore recommend supporting them 1.2 m (4 ft) off the ground. The best way to do this is to place them on a framework of metal piping. Any number of cages can be placed side by side on this framework, taking care to leave about 30 cm (1 ft) between cages.

To break up the stark outline of rows of suspended cages, it is desirable to leave a space large enough to plant a tree after every fourth or fifth cage. Not only will this provide shade, but it will help to give a more natural feeling to what is otherwise a most unnatural setting for macaws. Some people are inclined to set up suspended cages for parrots as though they are going in for battery chicken farming and the result is a sort of psittacine housing development with no green or pleasant areas, the equivalent of a human concrete jungle. Suspended cages can be excellent if emphasis is placed on making them attractive places for the birds to live in and comfortable for the keeper to work in.

If the cages are as high as 1.2 m (4 ft) off the ground, food and water containers must be placed just below the floor of the cage. They should be contained in a welded mesh tray and two holes, slightly smaller than the size of the containers, should be cut in the welded mesh of the floor so that the birds can reach the food and water. The trays should not be much higher than the height of the containers or the macaws will be able to upset them very easily. An important advantage of this system,

WELDED MESH RECOMMENDED FOR CAGES		
SPECIES	GAUGE	SIZE
Hyacinthine	10 g	7·5×1·25 cm or 5×2·5 cm (3×½ in or 2×1 in)
Blue and Yellow	12 g or 10 g	7·5×1·25 cm or 5×2·5 cm (3×½ in or 2×1 in)
Blue-throated	12 g or 10 g	7·5×1·25 cm or 5×2·5 cm (3×½ in or 2×1 in)
Scarlet	12 g or 10 g	7·5×1·25 cm or 5×2·5 cm (3×½ in or 2×1 in)
Green-winged	10 g	7·5×1·25 cm or 5×2·5 cm (3×½ in or 2×1 in)
Military	12 g or 10 g	7·5×1·25 cm or 5×2·5 cm (3×½ in or 2×1 in)
Buffon's	10 g	7·5×1·25 cm or 5×2·5 cm (3×½ in or 2×1 in)
Red-fronted	12 g	7·5×1·25 cm or 5×2·5 cm (3×½ in or 2×1 in)
Severe	14 g	5×2·5 cm or 2·5×2·5 cm (2×1 in or 1×1 in)
Other small macaws	16 g	2·5×2·5 cm or 2·5×1·25 cm (1×1 in or 1×½ in)

Blue and Yellow Macaws

Blue and Yellow Macaw on the point of hatching

When this Blue and Yellow Macaw chick was removed from the nest it weighed 325 g. Next morning, with the crop empty, its weight was 266 g

An eight-day-old Blue and Yellow Macaw that was being reared by Sun Conures (*Aratinga solstitialis*)

Blue and Yellow
Macaw

Blue and Yellow
Macaws at their
nest in Manu
National Park,
Peru

especially where aggressive macaws are concerned, is that one does not have to put one's hand inside the cage to replenish food and water.

Suspended cages must have a door at the front and the back, to enable perches to be replaced and to make catching easier. One door can be large enough for a person to enter if there is a floor support running the length of the cage. The nest box must be mounted on the outside. I would recommend a horizontal box, placed on a platform at the back of the cage. The nest box should be lined inside and out with strong welded mesh. It could otherwise become a means of escape.

Protection from the elements is extremely important. Cages should be sited to take advantage of natural windbreaks, such as trees. If these do not exist, rigid plastic sheeting should be pop-riveted to the framework of the cage. Strong winds can be extremely unpleasant, especially cold ones.

A roofing material – of whichever type is best suited to local conditions – should be used above the perch at the front of the cage, about 1 m (3 ft 4 in) in length. The roof at the back should extend about 2 m (6 ft 8 in), covering the perch and the nest box. In some locations this will not provide sufficient shade, and the use of a shade cloth above the roof

and at the side of the cage is therefore recommended.

Suspended cages are not suitable for cold, wet or excessively windy locations. Only a walk-in aviary with an enclosed shelter, or one sited partly in an enclosed building, can offer sufficient protection in such a site.

As the easiest way of cleaning suspended cages is to hose them, the cages should stand on a concrete base with a drainage channel running along their length. Cover the drainage outlets to prevent food and debris from falling into them, and do not site them below food trays.

It should be realized that large macaws, whether housed in suspended cages or walk-in aviaries, may be distracted from breeding by the presence of other large macaws in adjoining enclosures, whether or not these are of the same species. Visual separation for all or most of the length of the aviary is therefore desirable, especially beside the perches. Macaws may otherwise spend long periods clinging to the wire, either showing too much interest in their neighbors (and not in their partners) or exhibiting aggression.

Needless to say, double-wiring between adjoining aviaries is absolutely essential. Serious injuries to beak, tongue or feet can

In a hot climate, a false roof over an aviary helps to reduce the temperature within

occur if this important feature is neglected. It is a difficult matter to rectify after the aviary has been constructed. Even if you have seen aviaries which lack two divisions of wire and which are apparently successful, do not be tempted to copy them. Few people who have made this mistake are likely to broadcast the tragedies it has caused.

Combating theft
Thefts of parrots are, unfortunately, very common occurrences, especially of macaws because of their high value. All macaw owners should be aware of this and take precautions to prevent theft or to facilitate the recovery of stolen birds. *Before* building aviaries for macaws, consult a security company, as its staff can give advice on the best way to site aviaries to minimize the security devices used, and therefore the expense. Compared to the cost of a pair of macaws, the price of a security system is not so high.

Remember that many thefts occur in broad daylight, so if you have valuable birds, leave your property unattended as little as possible. If you have dogs patrolling the perimeter of your aviaries, keep them under a covered run so that a would-be thief cannot throw them poisoned or drugged meat.

Padlock aviary doors with locks of good quality and keep them padlocked day and night. It will be argued that a thief can cut through welded mesh – but this takes a lot longer than entering an unlocked door.

Even if your stolen birds are located, your problems may only just be beginning. How can you prove that the birds are yours? Bands are of little help as the first thing a thief will do is to cut off all bands. Tiny numbered microchips are increasingly being used to identify individual birds. These are implanted just below the skin and the number is read with the aid of a scanner. At present, their use is mainly limited to zoos and large private collections, but in the future microchips will surely be more widely used. Incidentally, the microchip can be quickly and easily removed by a qualified person, but because of the high cost of a scanner, a thief would be unlikely to own one and would therefore have no way of knowing if the bird carried an implant.

Keep good photographic records of all your macaws. Maintain a file of sharply focused close-up shots in the form of color transparencies or color prints. In large macaws, and especially in Green-wings, the pattern of feathers on the cheeks, and also the markings on the upper mandible, differ in individuals. Take photographs of the birds' heads to show these details, and also – if you have a good lens – close-up photographs of the feet. It has been suggested that the pattern of the scales on the feet is as significant in identifying individual macaws as are the fingerprints of humans.

Blue-throated Macaws

A strikingly beautiful bird, the Blue-throated is distinguished from the Blue and Yellow by the smaller unfeathered area on the face and by the blue throat

Blue-throated Macaws aged six and eight days

A parent-reared Blue-throated Macaw at 27 days old

The Blue-throated (formerly called the Caninde) Macaw, was unknown in aviculture until the early 1970s

5
Feeding for Health and Happiness

A nutritionist might argue – and some do – that all you need to keep your macaw in perfect health is pellets, or that these can be supplemented by up to 10 to 20 percent with other foods without upsetting the dietary balance. However, nutritionists consider only one aspect, the components of the food.

Macaws in a cage or aviary derive tremendous enjoyment from their food. They appreciate different textures, colors, tastes and shapes and receive necessary exercise from opening hard nuts, or amusement from extracting pips from grapes or peas from a pod. Holding a large item, such as a piece of corn cob or a whole carrot, also gives them pleasure.

How can the living enzymes and natural vitamins found in such foods as sprouted sunflower seed or mung beans, corn cobs, juicy oranges and entirely natural foods such as mangoes and the fruits of palm trees be contained in processed food such as pellets? There is no substitute for fresh natural foods.

I believe that food must be a major source of contentment in a macaw's life: that it should keep the bird happy as well as healthy. As an aviculturist, one of my greatest pleasures is to watch my birds enjoying the foods with which I present them, to share their anticipation not only at feeding time but at any time throughout the day when I might have items from the kitchen, such as the tops of red or green peppers which have gone into a casserole, or extra chicken cooked for those that crave animal protein; make no mistake – macaws do fall into this category.

Right from the start, macaw owners must think of their birds as omnivorous, that is, creatures which feed on almost anything edible and suitable. In the case of macaws, this quite often includes items which are definitely not advisable. Macaws are all too willing to experiment – those who look after these birds must be constantly on the alert to keep dangerous items away from them. Macaws do not fall into the large category of parrots which are only granivorous and frugivorous, that · is, eating only seeds and fruit; they need and relish a much wider variety of items.

Suitable foods can be placed in several categories. First are the fruits and vegetables which form the mainstay of their diet in the wild. Recommended fruits are apples, pears, oranges, grapes, bananas, mangoes, papayas, apricots, strawberries, kiwifruit, sweet grapefruit and cactus fruits. Those with stones (pits) in the center, such as peaches and plums, are good but most macaws will discard the fleshy part to reach the kernel, and therefore there may be no point in feeding any other part. Note that the kernels of stones from fruits such as peaches are considered to be toxic. I doubt that a single stone once or twice a week could do any harm, but do not feed more than this. Berry fruits, such as blueberries, blackcurrants, redcurrants and gooseberries, are also relished.

Do not forget the valuable wild harvest of berries and rose hips, provided that the area from which they are gathered is known not to have been sprayed with any toxic preparation. Macaws relish the berries of European hawthorn (*Crataegus monogyna*) and elder

Macaw-proof food containers. This stainless steel feeding tray has a piece of metal soldered to it. This is secured to the front of the aviary by means of a clip

(many species of *Sambucus* are found in most parts of the world), among others. Any fruit suitable for human consumption can, of course, be offered to macaws, as well as some which are not eaten by humans, such as the fruits of palm trees. The macaws in my care in the Canary Islands favor the small, fibrous orange fruits of the endemic *Phoenix canariensis*, and the *Arecastrum* from Brazil, above almost any other food.

Do not underestimate the value of dried fruits, which are a good source of protein, vitamins and minerals. Sultanas and raisins can be given dry but will be enjoyed even more after they are soaked for three or four hours; they are rich in iron and potassium. Figs can be offered fresh, or dried figs can be soaked; they too are valuable for their high iron content.

Of all the vegetables, fresh corn on the cob is generally the favorite. This is best cut into lengths of about 8 cm (3 in.) Peas in the pod, green beans, red and green peppers pimientos, carrots, zucchinis and tomatoes are all enjoyed raw. Cucumber will be eaten by some birds. Cooked beetroot and potato can also be offered. A number of kinds of beans can be given when they are beginning to sprout, when their vitamin content is many times higher than when fed dry; whether fed soaked or dry their protein content is double that of most cereals and even more than that of meat or eggs. Beans are also low in carbohydrate and fat, unlike seeds

such as sunflower. Suitable beans for sprouting for macaws are mung, chick pea (gorbanzo), black-eye, soya and haricot. Beans are the richest source of vegetable fiber and are also rich in iron, potassium and vitamins of the B group. An effort should therefore be made to persuade macaws to eat them. The beans should be soaked, drained and kept in a warm place or in a salad sprouter until they begin to sprout.

Dark green leaf vegetables are better than light green leaves as they have a higher vitamin content. Swiss chard, watercress, the leaves from brussels sprouts, cabbage and spring greens are excellent. Lettuce, including endive, kale and celery can also be offered.

Many weeds or wild plants are nutritionally excellent and also provide amusement or occupation. Again they must be gathered from areas known not to have been sprayed with insecticide and not from along the edges of busy roads, as such plants may be contaminated with exhaust fumes from traffic. Large gardens and arable fields are good sources of wonderful foods such as chickweed, sow thistle and dandelion. The whole dandelion (*Taraxacum officinale*) can be fed; young leaves are especially relished. Seeding grasses are enjoyed by the smaller macaws.

Now we come to seeds; I would suggest that sunflower and/or safflower seed be fed in one container and a mixture of small seeds be fed in another. The trend these days seems to be towards feeding parrots in aviaries from one flat container which slides out. This may be very convenient for the keeper but it does not allow for much versatility in the diet. I prefer facilities for three or four food containers, and recommend stainless steel food containers which clip into a revolving panel.

Sunflower seed
There are a number of different types of sunflower, grown in many different areas of the world, and thus the analyses of different seeds

vary considerably. However, most sunflower seed is a good source of protein; if this were not so, it would not be possible for so many parrots to have survived on little else. Recently an excellent small striped sunflower seed has been developed in the United States, reputedly especially for feeding to parrots. Its kernel is as full as that of many larger types and its oil content is said to be less.

In general, how should sunflower seed be chosen and bought? I would suggest that it be obtained from a reputable importer or dealer in bird seed, preferably one who is long established and pays particular attention to the cleanliness of the seed. Good seed costs more because it has been cleaned several times. It is a false economy to buy cheap seed; it will not have been cleaned properly and may be contaminated with some substance which is deadly to parrots. Regrettably, I know several people who have seen all their parrots die a sudden and distressingly painful death as the result of consuming contaminated sunflower seed.

On obtaining a new batch of sunflower seed, feed it to one bird only if there is any doubt about its cleanliness or origin. Test it for germination by soaking a sample

for 24 hours, and then rinse it and keep it in a warm place. In fresh seed of good quality at least 90 percent will germinate. If less than 60 percent germinates, its food value is low and it may be very stale. Look also at the plumpness of the kernel; some large seeds have very small kernels and are therefore of poor value economically and nutritionally.

I prefer to feed all sunflower seed after it has been soaked for 24 hours and is just commencing to sprout, because (a) soaking and rinsing afterwards remove most of the dirt; (b) the seed is easier to digest, especially for young birds; (c) most important, its food value is greatly increased, especially the vitamin content. However, in localities where the humidity is very high, only a small quantity, which will be consumed immediately, should be given at one time, as the seed could attract a fungus within a few hours.

I believe that all young birds should be offered soaked or sprouted sunflower seed, not dry seed, and that the longer this is continued (preferably indefinitely) the better it is for them. There are some very stubborn birds which have perhaps existed for many years on a diet of sunflower seed alone. If soaked sunflower seed is

Whole walnuts should be offered to Hyacinthines and all macaws larger than and including the Red-fronted. For smaller species the walnuts must be cracked

introduced gradually, and then sprouted, some of the deficiencies of a totally dry seed diet will be rectified. When offering sprouted seed, note that the sprouts should be small, no more than about 6 mm (¼ in.), and that most parrots will not eat them when the sprouts are longer than about 12 mm (½ in.). This means that sprouted seed must be removed each day.

Safflower seed, which is less than half the size of sunflower seed, and white, is offered instead of sunflower seeds by some breeders. Few offer macaws a mixture of small dry seeds, yet these are often relished; they also provide occupation as it takes much longer to eat the equivalent volume, compared with sunflower seed, for example. Suitable seeds are canary, oats, buckwheat and millet; hemp should be limited as most parrots soon become addicted to it. It is, however, an excellent winter food.

Nuts

Nuts are an essential part of the diet of large macaws, which derive great pleasure from cracking Brazils, walnuts and hazelnuts. These will need to be cracked by the keeper for the smaller species, and almonds should be cracked for most macaws, as their smooth shells make them difficult to open. Many macaws will pick peanuts in the shell out of a wide variety of items, as being the most favored of all. Buy only peanuts suitable for human consumption, as those of inferior quality or those incorrectly stored could be the source of a deadly fungus. Peanut kernels which have been boiled, thereby removing any health hazard, are also relished. I would recommend that all large macaws each receive at least three large nuts in their shells daily, the number being limited only by the cost. Pinenuts are also good if they have not been kept too long; a few should be tested from each new batch.

It may be significant that two of the most successful breeders of macaws I know, Harry Sissen in the United Kingdom and Mrs. Charlie Forker in Florida, feed large quantities of whole nuts to their birds, and also pieces of coconut. Brazil nuts form part of the diet of some macaws in the wild; these are the only natural food we can provide for our macaws (except for those fortunate enough to reside where palm trees grow), and are a favorite item which provides occupation and beak exercise. It is expensive to feed many whole nuts to a large collection of macaws, but if these foods result in greater contentment and in even one more young bird being reared, the cost is not to be counted. The success of the two breeders mentioned is not, of course, directly related to the number of nuts in the diet but reflects the fact that those who really care about their birds and give them what they need *and* like, rather than what is quick, cheap or convenient, have the right attitude towards their birds, that is, they are totally in sympathy with them.

Charles Munn (1988a) commented: ". . . the general impression we have about macaw diets at this point is that they are extremely varied – running the gamut in hardness and palatability from small, soft figs to large, hard palm nuts and bitter seeds of *Cedrela odorata*." He noted the macaws' tendency to eat the seeds of slightly unripe fruits, presumably because if they waited until the fruits were ripe there would be too much competition from other fruit-eaters. In the case of *Cedrela*, which is mahogany, however, the seeds are so bitter that no other bird or animal will eat them.

Animal protein

Macaws consume animal protein when they have the opportunity. Estudillo Lopez (1986) describes Military Macaws eating freshwater snails found along river banks, and gave this interesting account of the activities of a group of 15 Scarlet Macaws in Chiapas. They were in a pool close to the banks of the River Lacantun:

. . . creating a great racket. The pool was left over from the rainy

This coarse mineral block is ideal for large macaws

chances are it will go for meat; the craving which many parrots show for meat is almost certainly due to the lack of animal protein in most captive diets. Cooked lean meat is recommended, as are chop bones with a little meat adhering to them, and chicken carcasses. The latter are a great treat for the large macaws and many will eat every part of the carcass, including the bones and their marrow.

Many human foods are greatly enjoyed, are of value nutritionally and help to add variety to the diet. Items cooked in fat should be avoided, however, and also avocado pears, butter, margarine and salted items. Suitable foods include crackers, cheese, yogurt, muesli and other cereals such as cornflakes.

season, when the level of the water of the river dropped, leaving it cut off. At the beginning I thought they were bathing, for scarlet macaws are very fond of this. In the dry season they look for pools to refresh themselves in, but to my surprise, they were not bathing at all, but eating the fish which had been trapped in the pool when the water level descended.

Animal protein is good for large macaws and also any which are feeding young. Macaws in the wild sometimes consume lizards and even small dead animals when the opportunity presents itself. If you allow a pet macaw to help itself from your plate at mealtimes, the

Minerals
The need that macaws and other parrots have for minerals is often overlooked. Mineral blocks and mineral/vitamin additives can be found in most large pet stores. However, only extra strong blocks can be used for the large macaws; others will be crumbled up like chalk. It is a simple matter to make one's own, using calcium carbonate, mineral grit, limestone grit or pigeon grit and a little cement and water. A few

Orange is a favorite food of most large macaws, but they will ignore it if it is peeled. They extract the juice with tongue and mandible, then tip back the head

experiments will need to be carried out regarding the correct quantity of cement to be used for each species; obviously Hyacinthines and Green-wings will need more if the resulting block is to be firm enough. The mixture can be poured into sections cut from plastic bottles; a piece of wire from which to hang the block can be set within it. When the block has hardened, the outer plastic mold is removed.

A mineral/vitamin additive should be sprinkled on soft food or a very small amount placed inside a favorite item of fruit. It is pointless adding such supplements to seed as most is lost when the seed is husked.

In the wild, macaws are known to congregate on clay banks to eat clay. Charles Munn (1988a) states:

> This clay might help absorb or filter out these distasteful or toxic compounds [from seeds and from the tannin in the pulp of unripe fruit] from their diet, much as vintners use clays to filter out some of the bitter tannins from red wine, and highland Indians in the Andes grind clay with the bitter wild potato to bind toxic alkaloids and thus render the poisonous tuber edible.

(Analysis of the nutrients and secondary compounds in macaw foods, minerals and clays was being carried out by Munn's associates.)

Before leaving the subject of food, mention should be made of feeding frequency. Because macaws look forward to their food so much and because food can deteriorate quickly in extremes of temperature, it is better to feed a smaller amount three or four times a day rather than give all the food for the day at once. Most macaws tend to search for their favorite item; many will throw out everything else to find a peanut or a piece of orange. Knowledge of the preference of individuals can therefore save much waste, as the favored item can be placed on top. If only one feeding is given, the delicacies will be consumed at once, with nothing to look forward to for the rest of the day. Alternatively, the basic food mixture can be given in the morning and nuts and fruits at midday and late afternoon. The eagerness with which these foods will be greeted will more than compensate for the little extra work involved.

Food and water containers

Careful consideration must be given to food and water containers for large macaws – more so than for any other parrot. Most containers must be screwed or clipped into position.

A number of ideas are used to prevent dishes from being overturned, such as feeders placed in a wire cage below floor level. The macaw has to put its head through the opening to reach the container below. This is not ideal for large macaws as they cannot easily reach the food unless the opening is large, in which case the wire cage must be made to fit the food container exactly or the bird may push it out of reach. Stainless steel dishes can be used with a good design of this type. They are the most hygienic and hard wearing, but too light in weight for ordinary feeding shelves unless clipped or screwed into position.

The larger pet stores sell special feeding cups which can be used in the cage of a single large macaw. The size is not always adequate and if a variety of foods are offered it is advisable to use perhaps three cups for food and one cup for water. Some types of food containers, such as those which fit into a stainless steel ring, are not suitable, because unless the container fits very tightly into the ring the macaw will remove it within seconds.

When designing aviaries, do not place feeding shelves above eye level. A casual glance as you pass the aviary should enable you to keep an eye on the contents of the food containers.

6
Disease and General Care

Large macaws are potentially extremely long-lived birds, with a life span to equal that of human beings. Unfortunately, most do not realize this potential. However, the chances of captive-bred birds living for 50 or 60 years, or even more, are far greater than is the case with wild-caught macaws, many of which, when imported, are diseased or suffering from severe dietary deficiencies which will later result in disease. Trade in wild-caught macaws will soon belong in the past. This fact, coupled with the great strides in avian veterinary medicine which were made in the 1980s, and which can confidently be expected to progress much further in the 1990s, should help to ensure a longer lifespan for captive macaws. Even the smallest species could live for 40 years, possibly more.

The key to longevity lies in four aspects of the birds' care: emotional welfare, correct diet, good hygiene and suitable accommodation. The first, emotional welfare, is even more important than for most other parrots, because macaws (like cockatoos and Gray Parrots) are intelligent and very sensitive. Even if every other aspect of their care is correct, if the bird is unhappy it will not thrive. It will be unhappy if deprived of contact with its own kind (not necessarily its own species) or a close relationship with a human being, which is the equivalent. In a compatible pair of macaws, the bond is extremely strong and the birds are seldom more than a few inches apart. A solitary macaw, or one with an incompatible mate, is not a happy creature and is thus more susceptible to stress, and therefore disease, than a bird which is content. An adult macaw which never screams and shouts is not a happy bird. Macaws are naturally noisy; loud vocalizations are the normal method of expressing themselves.

Feather plucking
The condition of the plumage is a good indication of the state of mind, and often the state of health, of a macaw. When stressed, the birds often resort to plucking themselves. This undesirable habit usually starts with the removal of the feathers from the breast or with chewing the tail feathers. In large macaws, one member of a pair will often pluck the head feathers of its mate or young. If the extent of this is not severe, it may have little significance. Indeed, I have seen a film of a pair of Scarlet Macaws with their two young in the wild, before and after they left the nest, and at least one of the youngsters had the feathers of the crown plucked! All parrots preen their chicks, and in macaws, which are very affectionate towards their young and mate, this behavior sometimes becomes exaggerated and leads to plucking.

However, there is always a reason for a macaw plucking its own feathers or for *severely* denuding its mate. Many people believe that this is the result of poor feeding, or an excess of sunflower seed. Perhaps, rarely, this is the case. I believe, however, that the problem is almost always emotional. In a single bird one often needs to look no further than the fact that the macaw is sexually mature and extremely frustrated at being unable to breed. The sex hormones produced by the gonads (testes in the male and a single ovary in the female) are very potent and can easily change a bird's behavior. Provide a compatible mate and the fleeting habit may cease very quickly.

On the other hand, a large macaw could live in a permanent state of stress if it was afraid of its companion. It would be extremely unlikely to breed. Imagine how unhappy you would be if shut up permanently in a small room with someone you were afraid of or detested. You, too, would resort to biting your nails (the equivalent of feather plucking).

If you suspect incompatibility to be the prime cause of plucking, separate the two birds for several weeks or months, spray them daily or as often as possible with warm water (rain or tap water), give a varied diet containing fresh fruits and vegetables daily and a little vitamin B to improve the quality of the new feathers. Vitamin B is available in a number of forms suitable for parrots, such as brewer's yeast, available in all pet shops. This can be sprinkled on food. There are also palatable drops which can be added to water or to bread and milk or some other favored soft food. A veterinarian can advise as to what is available. There will be no improvement until the bird molts; however in severe cases, the feather follicles may be destroyed, in which case normal feather growth is impossible.

If there is substantial improvement in the plumage, the new feathers not being removed, it indicates that the macaw is no longer stressed. If the two birds are reunited, do not appear compatible, and one or both resumes plucking itself, they should be separated permanently and found new mates. If one bird is plucking the other (and perhaps itself as well), however, they may be perfectly compatible and likely to breed. It is well worth giving them the chance as the activity involved in rearing a family often distracts the plucker to the degree that it is cured – for a while, at least.

The need to gnaw

Large macaws (like cockatoos) have a great need to gnaw in order to find some activity for their beaks. It is distressing to see some macaws kept in cages with plastic or metal perches, totally denied the opportunity to bite at anything except their own tails. Whether kept in a cage or aviary, macaws *must* be allowed to gnaw wood, pine cones, nuts and their shells, fresh branches from deciduous or pine trees or anything else safe that provides occupation and amusement. Caged macaws will find endless amusement in offcuts of untreated wood, clean stones, leather dog chews, cardboard boxes and fruit juice cartons. Do not provide chains, string or any fabric which might become wound around the neck or foot.

Caging and clipping

For the reasons already outlined, I consider it unethical to keep single specimens of the large macaws caged as pets. I accept, however, that a young bird may be obtained and kept in this way until a second is purchased. There is no harm at all in the bird becoming tame and attached to its owner, provided that it is paired up by the time it is two years old. The large macaws

An essential requirement for all macaws is wood for gnawing. These Hyacinthines enjoy chewing their eucalyptus perches. Perches must be renewed regularly or fresh branches, such as pine, offered as often as possible

The correct way to hold a macaw so that its beak is immobilized. Place thumb and forefinger on either side of the lower mandible

however, because there is so much trouble the birds can get into, such as chewing through power cables.

Personally, I hate to deprive a macaw of its powers of flight by clipping one wing, but in some circumstances this is advisable or necessary. It is recommended that all the primaries and secondaries of *one wing only* be cut, except the outer primary, which is retained solely for the sake of appearance. Clipping only one wing has the effect of unbalancing the bird completely. A careful watch must be kept for molting and new feather growth, as with only three primaries on the clipped wing a macaw is capable of perfect flight.

Transporting macaws
If you have to transport a macaw by road, rail or air, and you have not done this before, buy or make the traveling container well before the journey. The larger pet suppliers sell traveling boxes for dogs and cats which are also excellent for macaws. They can be obtained in sizes to suit all species of macaw and are constructed of strong plastic with a metal or plastic-coated door. Slight modifications are necessary before these boxes are suitable for the large macaws. A strong perch should be fitted about 8 cm (3 in.) off the floor. A hole can be drilled in each side of the box and a screw fitted through these and into each end of the perch to hold it in place. The ventilation slits in each side of the box should be covered from the

mature slowly and if raised with people they usually remain quite dependent on them, emotionally, for about 18 months. After this their personalities become more forceful. Small macaws, on the other hand, show independence and forcefulness at five or six months, when they are seldom distinguishable from adults, in their physical aspect or in their behavior.

Caged macaws should be let out of the cage every day. This is especially important for the large species which have a great need to flap their wings, even if they are unable to fly. Far better, however, to have a room devoid of ornaments or valuables, in which they can run about, explore or fly if they wish. The alternative, with a tame bird which can be handled easily, is to house it in an aviary during the day and bring it into the home in the evening, especially if the members of the family are present only in the evening. Out in the aviary it can be supplied with fresh branches for chewing, have access to rain and sunshine, and fly and climb as the mood takes it. Many macaws will not fly in aviaries because these accommodations are not large enough, but they will often fly in a house. Periods of freedom in a house must be strictly supervised,

A plastic carrying kennel for dogs and cats is ideal for transporting macaws. Made in two halves, it is easy to unscrew in order to fit a perch in the base

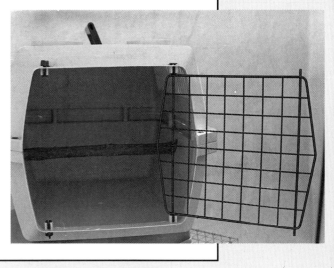

Above and below: two other types of carrying boxes intended for dogs. The lower one has been adapted for use by large macaws by fitting panels of welded mesh inside over the plastic bars

for three or four days, in case of delays or misrouting.

When traveling by car, even if your macaw's cage will fit inside the vehicle, the bird will be quieter and travel more securely in a traveling box. The majority of parrots seem perfectly content inside a box, even on long journeys. If a macaw is to travel by air or rail, advise the carrier of the size and weight of the container in advance, to ensure that it meets with the appropriate regulations. Add the weight of the bird to that of the box.

A pair of large macaws should not travel in the same box, even although they are normally kept together. If upset or frightened, one might attack the other. For a very nervous bird the front of the box should be covered with a cloth; this must be fine enough to allow enough light through for the bird to be able to feed.

inside with welded mesh, the top and bottom of which is covered by a strip of aluminum and pop-riveted to the side of the box. When confined for several hours, macaws may make use of their powerful beaks out of boredom or frustration, even if they are not normally destructive. A strong padlock is also useful and may reduce the chance of theft or escape.

Unless the carrier insists otherwise, it is usually better to provide plenty of fruit, such as oranges, apples and grapes, rather than include a water container which will probably get upset, resulting in the floor of the box being damp throughout the journey. Birds sent by rail or air should be given enough seed to last

Spraying with water
Some people, while otherwise very sensitive to the requirements of their macaws, fail to realize the importance of spraying them. All parrots need water on their plumage to keep it in perfect condition, with a high gloss. Small species can bathe in their water containers but this is impossible for most macaws, which must therefore be sprayed at least twice a week. A plant mister is suitable for the purpose. Young birds, just weaned, and adults not used to being sprayed should receive a light misting on the first few occasions. Spraying can take place in a warm room (bathroom or kitchen) or outside on a warm day. A garden hose can be used with a finger placed over the end to deflect the flow of water into a spray, rather than a jet. The latter could cause shock.

Never leave a bird in the hot sun to dry; parrots must be protected from strong sun, and macaws do not sunbathe, unlike some parrots. They do rainbathe, however, and a shower of rain after a period of drought will cause them to react in an ecstasy of delight, spreading

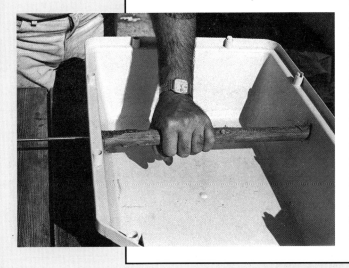

their wings to catch more drops of rain on their plumage. Those kept indoors can be placed outside for a few minutes in a light shower of rain on a warm day. Even before they are weaned, young macaws will clearly show their pleasure and excitement at experiencing water on their plumage. Do not neglect this aspect of their care. It gives them so much enjoyment and keeps them feather-perfect!

Cleanliness and hygiene
Disease usually originates from unhygienic surroundings (where molds and bacteria thrive), from wild birds and from animals or insects, such as mice or cockroaches, which are carrying disease. Alternatively, disease is often dormant in the bird and will surface if the bird is stressed. New acquisitions in a collection are potentially a great danger to those already in residence. A quarantine period of four or five weeks is recommended, but realistically a new parrot would have to be kept apart for several months to be fairly sure it was not incubating a serious disease. It could be years – or never – before one was discovered to be a carrier of a disease which could spread to all others in the collection, or to only some of them. Susceptibility to certain diseases or strains of a disease may vary according to the species of parrot. Macaws, as a group, are not normally susceptible to psittacine beak and feather syndrome (loss of all plumage, caused by a virus) but they are susceptible to psittacosis, Pacheco's disease and skin herpes.

Psittacosis
More correctly known as chlamydiosis, this disease can affect many species of birds, including feral pigeons. Many pet birds are carriers, but they show no symptoms, are perfectly healthy and, unless severely stressed, are unlikely to shed *Chlamydia psittaci*, the agent responsible. It has been described as something between a virus and a bacterium (a pathogen). However, some strains of the disease are much more serious and are resistant to antibiotics.

Although many Budgerigars and Cockatiels are carriers, they seldom die from chlamydiosis, whereas the disease is often fatal in macaws and Amazons. Anyone who obtains a recently imported wild-caught macaw is advised to take it to a veterinarian to be treated against psittacosis. All quarantine stations in the United States, and some elsewhere, give tetracycline to parrots being quarantined. Carriers which have been treated may show no symptoms but the stress of transport and a new environment (i.e., the home of the unsuspecting purchaser) could cause them to start shedding *Chlamydia*. There are no consistent symptoms; however, a blood test has now been developed that can detect the disease, and only a few drops of blood are required. Another method, involving smearing nasal or ocular exudate on microscope slides, will often (although not always) reveal if a bird is infected.

Joel D. Murphy (1989), an avian veterinarian in Florida, suggests: "When you acquire a parrot you should consider the bird a carrier of psittacosis until proven otherwise." If the bird is a pet going into a family, he recommends that it should have a psittacosis profile completed with the new purchase examination (physical examination, X-rays, blood tests and Gram's stain), especially if there are already other birds in the household. If there is any evidence of psittacosis, the bird should be treated for a minimum of 45 days. There is little risk to humans because birds do not usually shed *Chlamydia* once the treatment has commenced.

It should be noted that usually only avian veterinarians will be familiar with the examinations and tests described by Joel Murphy. It is therefore essential to find one who has the necessary experience *before* you purchase your first macaw. Managers of local pet shops or the secretary of the local cage-bird society should be able to recommend an avian veterinarian.

Chlamydia psittaci can be detected from cloacal swabs of infected birds by using the commercially available ELISA test kit. The results are rapid and specific, but samples must be collected for several days from an individual bird, and several samples (cloacal swabs) are needed from birds in a flock.

Under the name of psittacosis, chlamydiosis often receives sensational treatment by the press because it can be transmitted to humans. However, in humans the disease is very easily cured with the use of tetracycline although it may be potentially dangerous for persons who are elderly, sick or immuno-deficient (e.g., AIDS patients). If you have flulike symptoms, a high temperature and a fever and find difficulty in breathing after any exertion such as walking upstairs, you should consult a doctor immediately, providing the information that psittacosis is a possibility.

Remember that good hygiene will help to prevent the spread of the disease. The dust from dried feces carrying *Chlamydia psittaci* can apparently remain infectious for months.

Cloacal papilloma
A clinical condition seen in neotropical parrots, and especially in macaws, is cloacal papilloma. So far, the Green-winged and the Blue and Yellow Macaw are the species most commonly affected. Scott McDonald (1989) reported that he had never seen the condition in miniature macaws or in the Hyacinthine. Affected birds have lesions in the cloaca which, in advanced cases, resemble a prolapse. In the early stages single or multiple "stalks" can be seen as tiny raised granules. There may be just one small cluster or hundreds of them over the cloacal lining. Eventually this abnormal tissue becomes so pronounced that it is pushed out of the vent when the bird eliminates feces. In severe cases the papilloma is so large that

This beautiful Blue and Yellow Macaw died two days after this photograph was taken – a victim of a virus, probably Pacheco's disease. It was kept in a private collection and the owner had housed a young, newly obtained macaw next to it, which, apparently, was a carrier of Pacheco's disease

it cannot be retracted.

To examine for this condition, the end of a cotton-tipped applicator (cotton bud or Q-tip) should be gently introduced into the cloaca. The tip is pushed to one side and slowly withdrawn to ease out the cloacal lining on that side. The lining of the cloaca should be completely smooth; if it has a granulated appearance, the disease should be suspected. Clinical signs are loose droppings, straining to defecate, feces adhering around the vent and blood in the droppings. Surgery is recommended at the very early stage of the disease when the lesions are small and segregated.

Walter Rosskopf, a California veterinarian who has seen many cases, believes that the condition is highly infectious. The following experience of another veterinarian bears this out. In one collection eight pairs of macaws were examined and in each bird the cloaca seemed normal. The owner then purchased a Blue and Yellow

Macaw which was diagnosed as having cloacal papillomas several months later. One year later five of the original 16 birds showed clinical evidence of having cloacal papillomas.

Scott McDonald knew of two cases in which birds with mild to moderate lesions produced fertile eggs. In one case, both male and female had lesions. However, birds with severe lesions would not be able to copulate properly.

Parrot pox

A new vaccine, developed by Maine Biological Laboratories and distributed by California Avian Laboratory, protects parrots, including macaws, from this disease. This vaccine, administered by intramuscular injection, is one of the first commercially available vaccines for birds.

Pacheco's disease

One of the most serious diseases that can occur in macaws and other parrots, often reaching epidemic proportions, is Pacheco's disease, a virus disease related to the herpes virus. The symptoms are nonspecific and the course of the disease is so rapid that a macaw could die a few hours after the first signs of abnormality are noticed. Stress caused by a change of location often triggers shedding of the virus in the feces of carrier birds. This shedding is so heavy that all birds in contact with the carrier bird become ill. One problem is that when a carrier bird starts to shed the virus it does not look unwell and thus dozens of birds could become contaminated.

This is why quarantine for newly obtained birds is of vital importance. To be effective against this disease, however, the quarantine period of new birds would have to be twelve weeks. Any birds known to have been in contact with carriers would also have to be quarantined for this period of time. Harrison and Harrison (1986) state that the incubation period in the Green-cheeked Amazon, following experimental infection, is three to four days and that contact birds die after six days.

Identification of Pacheco's disease is not easy; virus isolation is frequently necessary and the final diagnosis is made by blood testing. A vaccine against Pacheco's disease, administered by intramuscular injection, has been developed by Maine Biological Laboratories (distributed by California Avian Laboratory).

Papovavirus

On its discovery the first known papovavirus was called Budgerigar fledgling disease because it was found to cause high mortality in chicks of this species. However, it soon became apparent that the disease could affect any psittacine. Florida veterinarian Dr. Joel Murphy estimated that it was the cause of death in 31 percent of parrot chicks being hand-reared. Papovavirus is not diagnosed in the vast majority of chicks that die of this disease because it can be determined only by histopathic examination (examination of the body tissues). This is expensive, few veterinarians are qualified histologists and, unfortunately, many breeders make no effort to ascertain cause of death until fatalities reach epidemic proportions. This can occur with papovavirus.

Dr. Murphy (1987) commented: "Macaws seem to be the most resistant to the disease and often survive with intensive therapy. Sun Conures seem to be the least resistant and often die first in an outbreak involving different species."

As it happened, my only encounter with papovavirus involved four macaw chicks of a small species and one Sun Conure. They were being hand-reared with about 30 or 40 other parrot chicks. It became apparent when they were about a month old that there was something wrong with the macaws. They bruised very easily, especially on the head. This and hemorrhaging are typical symptoms of papovavirus. They were extremely thin and abnormally slow to feather. When the feathers eventually erupted they were very dry and lacked luster. The same symptoms, except bruising, were seen in the Sun Conure. The four macaws and the conure were isolated in a building away from all other chicks. When they were nearly four months old (and featherless) the decision was made to sacrifice the Sun Conure, which was the worst affected, and one of the macaws, and the diagnosis was confirmed. However, by six months the three remaining macaws were completely feathered. Weaning was abnormally slow and was not accomplished until they were eight months old. They then looked perfect and all three were given to one person to keep as pets.

Jack M. Gaskin, an American veterinarian, carried out research into papovavirus infections. He had a Nanday Conure which had survived an outbreak which killed many parrot chicks. At two years old she was serologically positive but outwardly normal in every way. For over six months she was kept with a male which remained serologically positive to the virus. At seven weeks old the chick they produced was serologically negative. Nevertheless, birds which have a history of infection should not be used for breeding.

Gaskin described the clinical signs of affected chicks as weakness, loss of appetite, slow emptying of the crop, regurgitation, subcutaneous hemorrhage (producing a bluish coloration of the skin) and abdominal distension. Postmortem findings included pallor of muscles, fluid in the heart sac, enlarged heart, enlarged liver with a spotted or mottled appearance, enlarged spleen, pale or congested kidneys and occasionally ascites. Histological lesions included enlargement of the nuclei of cells in a variety of organs, with attendant pale viral inclusion bodies and multifocal to disseminated liver destruction (Gaskin, 1988).

Proventriculus dilatation syndrome
Initially called macaw wasting

disease, this is another virus disease which was not recognized until the early 1980s. So called because it was first diagnosed in macaws, it can affect most psittacine species. The virus causes paralysis of the proventriculus (first stomach). This means that the food, instead of being passed quickly to the intestines, remains for a long time in the stomach and is not properly digested when it does reach the intestines. Undigested seed and other food can be seen in the feces of affected birds. (Of course, this symptom is not peculiar to this condition.) Because of the extended period that the food remains in the stomach and intestines, bacteria grow, resulting in a bacterial infection which may be fatal.

As this is a virus disease, antibiotics will not cure it, but they should be used to prevent or treat secondary bacterial infections (Murphy, 1988). The disease can be diagnosed by a series of X-rays which will show the dilated stomach (a single X-ray showing this feature is not necessarily significant). Affected birds will gradually become thin and depressed. Treatment is rarely successful. At Murphy Animal and Bird Hospital in Florida the treatment success rate was nil with macaws, Sun Conures, Cockatiels and Eclectus Parrots, 10 percent success was achieved with Gray Parrots and 100 percent with cockatoos. Treatment consisted of intravenous antibiotics, medication and feeding. As the virus apparently leaves the bird's body after some time, there is a chance that the affected bird will survive if it has time to fight the virus and repair the damage to its nervous system.

7

Aviary Reproduction

Experience in breeding parrots should be gained with prolific and rapidly maturing species such as Budgerigars, lovebirds and Cockatiels. In this way the basics can be learned quickly. Even those with some experience would be wise to purchase a couple of dwarf macaws, as they mature early and some pairs prove very prolific. The young are always in demand as pets, and this income will help to fund the expensive project of breeding the large macaws. The financial outlay involved in setting up even two pairs is considerable, so most breeders finance this through the sale or exchange of young of other species.

Few people are prepared to buy young macaws of the large species and wait for them to mature, as this could take four to six years, or several years longer for wild-caught birds. The exception is the tame baby which is to be kept as a pet until it is old enough to breed. In this case it is advisable to buy two to prevent them from becoming imprinted on one person. Two young macaws will never be bored or lonely; they will play together (or squabble companionably) for hours on end. At an early age their sexes will be unknown – unless they have been sexed by chromosome examination – but one has the option to exchange one or purchase more birds in due course.

Be cautious about buying proven breeding pairs of the large macaws. Genuine pairs which have reared young are seldom available. After all, only in exceptional circumstances would someone wish to part with such valuable and wonderful birds. In the dwarf macaws, which mature early and are easier to breed, young birds are the best investment, in my opinion.

Small macaws, such as Illiger's, can theoretically be sexed as early as six months. This is not recommended, however, as mistakes are more likely to be made when very young birds are laparoscoped. It would be advisable to wait until a large macaw is 11 or 12 months old.

The laparoscope is the instrument generally used to perform this simple operation. The bird is first anesthetized and will be unconscious for only three or four minutes if gas is used. If an injected anesthetic is utilized, it will be in the region of an hour before the bird has fully regained consciousness. A small incision is made above one leg, between the ribs (which may or may not be closed later with one stitch), to admit the laparoscope. A light source is attached to this to give a view of the internal organs. An experienced veterinarian can normally locate the sex organs very quickly, and thus discover whether the bird has testes (a male) or ovaries (a female). He or she can also observe whether the bird is sexually mature and sexually active or whether there is some abnormality which could prevent it from breeding. It should be noted that surgical sexing is generally carried out only by specialist avian veterinarians.

Compatibility

The small macaws are usually quite easy to pair up, that is, they are usually compatible with the partner provided. The large macaws are, perhaps, the most difficult of all the parrots in this respect, especially if there are other macaws in sight.

The pair bond can be very, very strong in macaws. It is often touching to see the devotion of one bird to another and the way a male will defend his female, always keeping himself between the female and the enemy, whether real or imagined. A compatible pair will stay constantly side by side. If one or both members of a "pair" have many sheaths of unopened feathers on the head, they are not compatible. Preening is carried out for such long periods in a devoted pair that brittle feather sheaths are not in evidence for long.

Pairs which are not compatible may clash bills and argue a lot, especially over food. One may keep the other away until it has removed all the choice items. In this case, two feeders should be provided or one bird will never receive its fair share of nuts and oranges. The problem may be only a temporary one on introduction, with one bird initially trying to establish its dominance over the other. Or it may become a permanent condition, with the dominated bird obviously unhappy. Such partnerships should be split up because birds which are stressed, for whatever reason, are more susceptible to disease.

The harmony between a compatible pair is a joy to see. However, be warned! Two males or two females can form a bond which is just as strong and as hard to break as that of a male and female. One reason why captive breeding of the large macaws has progressed so much in the past decade is the advent of surgical sexing. Before this was available, there were probably more same-sex "pairs" of large macaws than of any other parrots.

Chromosomal sexing
Destined to be the method of choice of future breeders, chromosomal sexing will greatly benefit aviculture and conservation. It was pioneered in the United States by Dr. Marc Valentine, whose laboratory was the first to offer this as a commercial service.

This method of sexing is based on the fact that every bird has a particular number of chromosomes, present in pairs. (Parrots have 30 to 40 pairs.) One

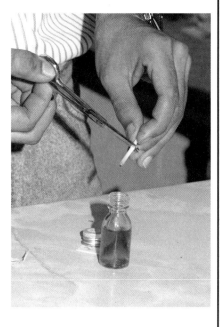

A blood feather being cut and placed in a bottle for shipment to a laboratory

of these pairs determines the sex. Once it has been established in a species which pair are the sex chromosomes, any bird can be sexed. In the female, one of this pair of chromosomes (called Z and W) is smaller than the other. In the male (both Z chromosomes) both are the same size. How does one obtain access to these chromosomes? In order to study them, cells which are in active division must be chosen. Such cells can be found in bone marrow, but one would have to kill the bird to obtain this! The alternative is to study the cells in the base of a growing feather.

Joshua, Hunt and Parker (1989) explain how this is done:

Cells from the blood feather are removed in sterile conditions and grown artificially to produce a large number of similar rapidly dividing cells. An inhibitor is added to stop the cells dividing when they have formed visible chromosomes. It is only while they are dividing that chromosomes can be observed. These are then stained and the number of chromosomes counted and paired up. This produces a karyotype, the name given to a particular set of chromosomes. From the appearance of the karyotype, the birds can be sexed.

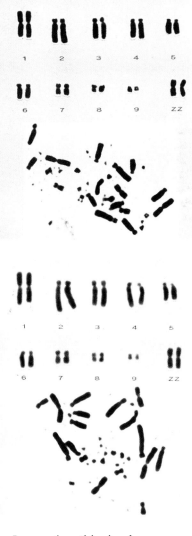

Karyotype and cell (below) of a Scarlet Macaw – produced by feather pulp culture and subsequent chromosome preparation

Karyotype and cell (below) of Illiger's Macaw

Irresponsible hybridizing

This practice has resulted in many hybrids being produced between a male Scarlet and a female Blue and Yellow. Such birds are known in the United States as Catalina Macaws. These hybrid macaws are purposely produced for those who want something different. Their value is as high or even higher than that of pure-bred macaws. In Europe there is no market for such hybrids, their production is usually accidental and their value is low; in fact, they are difficult to sell.

Breeding hybrids from species which are endangered or threatened in the wild is highly irresponsible. It is also fuel for those who are opposed to the keeping of birds. How can aviculturists claim to be conservationists, such people would rightly ask, when, instead of using endangered species to perpetuate the species, they are using them to produce hybrids for pet-bird owners who want something different? Some species of pheasants, for example, which are rare in captivity, have been so hybridized over several decades that it is now difficult to find pure stock. The same could happen with the large macaws unless breeders look to the future and give some thought to the consequences of pairing two species together in this way.

They are certainly not doing this in the United States, where names are given to the various crosses. The uninitiated may even believe that they are buying a true species. Producing hybrid macaws can only harm the reputation of aviculture. This fact should be reflected in a much lower value for hybrids; buyers should insist on this. It would appear to be the only means of reducing the numbers produced.

When searching for a mate for a macaw, an attempt should be made to find the same subspecies where this is well defined. In the Scarlet Macaw no subspecies have yet been named but the differences in birds from different parts of South or Central America are quite pronounced, so, there again, if it is

In practice, this simply means that one or two growing feathers, with blood still in the quill, must be removed from the bird to be sexed, and kept sterile until they reach the laboratory. Here the feather pulp is placed in a culture from which cells are grown.

This method has a number of important advantages. Stress to the bird to be sexed is minimal; no surgery is involved; young birds can be sexed even before they leave the nest. It is completely accurate when carried out by a skilled scientist familiar with the chromosomes of the species. A bonus is that the culture can be frozen and stored for years. It can then be thawed to yield living cells which may be grown for analysis. This could have important applications for endangered species.

possible, this factor should be taken into consideration.

Nest boxes

After a true pair has been set up in suitable accommodation, the next most important consideration is the nest box. In general, large macaws are not fussy about their nesting sites, possibly because in the wild such large birds will not easily find suitable sites unless they inhabit rocky hills or mountainsides. Many macaws nest in crevices in rocks because trees with large cavities are difficult to find. It has been known for macaws, which have not been provided with a box, to make a scrape on the aviary floor and incubate there.

Oblong nest boxes are recommended for the large macaws; here the female can incubate without damaging her tail and there is more room for the growing chicks to move about. In order to provide a darker interior and a greater feeling of security for the occupants, an entrance section at right angles to the main part of the box (creating an L-shape) can be made. This is not essential, but a darker interior may stimulate some pairs to breed.

Most macaws enter their nest box readily and many roost inside it every night whether or not they

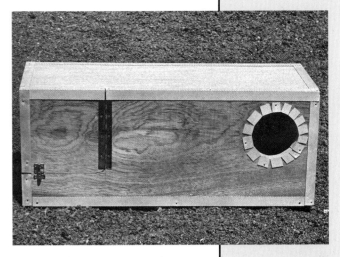

are breeding. Others use the nest for roosting only before and during the breeding period.

The strength of a large macaw's beak, especially when used in defense of its nest, must never be underestimated. For this reason it is essential to situate the next box or barrel where it can be inspected without entering the aviary. However, this alone does not solve the problem of nest inspection, as many macaws refuse to leave or move enough to enable one to observe eggs or chicks. The perfect design is therefore one which allows the nest entrance to be closed from outside the aviary so that when both birds leave to feed, the nest can be inspected without

Oblong nest boxes are recommended for the Red-fronted and all larger species of macaw. Note how all the edges are reinforced with metal

The correct way to mount a barrel, allowing nest inspection from outside the aviary, is seen in the photograph on page 52. In the enclosure seen here, nest inspection cannot be accomplished from outside the aviary and is therefore almost impossible

Scarlet Macaws

Two-day-old chicks: right, a Scarlet and left, a Blue and Yellow Macaw

Scarlet Macaw aged eight weeks, weighing 944 g

The beauty of Scarlet Macaws has long made them among the most sought-after of the family, with the result that excessive trapping of birds from the wild has occurred

The wonderful array of colors found in even a single feather of a Scarlet is perhaps unmatched in any other macaw

Horizontal nest-box mounted outside the aviary

inside and out with welded mesh, the entrance should be protected with strips of metal, and pieces of wood to gnaw at should be nailed inside (using small nails to ensure that they will not protrude too far or be in a dangerous position when the wood has been gnawed away). These should be replaced when convenient.

In upright boxes a means of access from the entrance to the base must be provided by either a strip of welded mesh or pieces of wood placed a few inches apart to form a ladder. Welded mesh should be bowed outwards slightly to prevent a bird from being trapped by a claw. Alas, such a sad

causing them any stress.

Because large macaws are so destructive and wooden nest boxes are expensive to replace, some breeders seek an alternative to wood, using metal barrels, for example. In my opinion, there is no suitable alternative to wood. Metal offers no protection from extremes of temperature; the interior will be unbearably hot or very cold according to the weather. Also, all parrots like to gnaw the interior of the nest and this often appears to be a stimulus to breeding. To preserve the life of a wooden nest box, it should be lined

A nesting barrel mounted outside the aviary

SUGGESTED SIZES FOR NEST BOXES (internal measurements)

Shape: oblong boxes are recommended for *Ara rubrogenys* and all larger species

Species	Length	Height	Width	Diameter of entrance hole
Hyacinthine	1–1·2 m (40–48 in)	47 cm (18 in)	47 cm (18 in)	25 cm (10 in)
Blue and Yellow	91–106 cm (36–42 in)	39 cm (15 in)	39 cm (15 in)	20 cm (8 in)
Scarlet	91–106 cm (36–42 in)	39 cm (15 in)	39 cm (15 in)	20 cm (8 in)
Military	91–106 cm (36–42 in)	39 cm (15 in)	39 cm (15 in)	20 cm (8 in)
Blue-throated	91–106 cm (36–42 in)	39 cm (15 in)	39 cm (15 in)	20 cm (8 in)
Green-winged	1 m (40 in)	39 cm (15 in)	39 cm (15 in)	25 cm (10 in)
Buffon's	1 m (40 in)	39 cm (15 in)	39 cm (15 in)	25 cm (10 in)
Red-fronted	1·2–1·3 m (48–52 in)	39 cm (15 in)	39 cm (15 in)	20 cm (8 in)

Shape: upright nest boxes are recommended for small macaws

Species	Base	Height	Diameter of entrance hole
Severe	31–36 cm (12–14 in)	61–76 cm (24–30 in)	8 cm (3 in)
Illiger's	"	"	"
Yellow-collared	"	"	"
Red-bellied	"	"	"
Hahn's	25–31 cm (10–12 in)	61 cm (24 in)	7 cm (2⅖ in)
Noble	"	"	"

accident must have occurred in the past to many birds. Bear in mind that the strips of wood must be inspected and replaced regularly; if completely gnawed away, a bird could be trapped inside. Also inspect the welded mesh ladder to ensure it remains in a safe condition.

The best lining for the base of the nest is wood shavings made from untreated wood. Ideally, these should be sterilized before use. A little Sevin Dust or some other safe insecticide can be mixed with the shavings to deter red mite and other insects.

Stimulating nonbreeding pairs
First, consider whether the birds feel secure in their surroundings. As macaws reproduce in countless different situations, one cannot make any hard and fast rules. However, if an apparently compatible adult pair have made no attempt to nest after three or four years, a change of scenery may work wonders. If they have been in a large aviary, move them to something quite different, such as a suspended cage. You might even consider moving them indoors, to a basement or barn. There might be something in the outdoor environment that is making them nervous – birds of prey, for example.

If they have been in a suspended cage and have not nested, move them to a well-sheltered aviary, perhaps with a large enclosed compartment. Aim to make the surroundings as different as possible, yet retain every feature likely to provide the birds with a sense of security. For macaws I do not approve of aviaries which are almost totally enclosed, as most macaws like to watch what is going on around them and may be bored if they cannot observe other birds or people, but see only plain walls. Another trick is to board up their nest box. What is no longer available suddenly becomes desirable and gnawing at the wood covering the entrance can also act as a stimulus to breeding.

An inadequate diet could inhibit reproduction, so ensure that the diet is nutritious and varied. A sudden increase in animal protein might stimulate reproduction, so start to feed cooked chicken carcasses, chop bones, monkey chow, dog biscuits and/or hard-boiled egg, whichever is preferred.

The importance of a compatible pair has already been discussed. However, remember that the birds may not be instantly compatible; they should be given a minimum of a year together to settle down, unless they quarrel continually to the point where one is stressed or not permitted to feed properly.

Another factor is whether the birds are old enough to reproduce. This can usually be determined when they are surgically sexed by observing the state of the ovaries or testes. Generally speaking, captive-bred macaws mature earlier than those captured in the wild, and small macaws mature more rapidly than large species. One captive-bred Hyacinthine produced fertile eggs when only four years old – but this may have been exceptional. Green-wings possibly take longer to mature than Hyacinthines. The small macaws can be expected to breed when three years old and Blue and Yellows may start breeding when only four (if captive-bred). However, compared to breeders of Budgerigars, macaw owners need a lot of patience!

Signs that nesting is imminent are that the birds inspect the nest, spending more time than usual within the nest box, and that they become noisier and more aggressive. Copulation is not necessarily an indication; some pairs, especially Hyacinthines, will copulate when closely observed, and yet this has absolutely no relevance to an intention to reproduce.

The female usually stays almost permanently inside the nest a few days before she starts to lay. She shapes the nest litter into a depression. During this period the male feeds her inside the nest, which she leaves briefly a couple of

Green-winged Macaws

The Green-winged is the third largest of the macaws and one of the most intelligent

Green-winged Macaw aged two and a half weeks, hatched at Loro Parque, Tenerife

At the age of 41 days, most Green-winged chicks are becoming affectionate and sweet-tempered

Only compatible pairs of macaws, such as these Green-winged, indulge in constant mutual preening

times a day. This behavior is also true of the incubation period, although some females will leave the nest at any disturbance. Some males will spend much time in the nest with the female, although it is unlikely that the males take any part in incubation. Often food consumption drops markedly at this time.

Clutch sizes and incubation periods are given in the sections covering individual species. Incubation normally commences when the first egg is laid, which means chicks usually hatch at intervals of three days.

Macaw eggs and incubation

The eggs of macaws are normally much glossier than those of other parrots. Many of them have the appearance of china, so shiny are they, and might even mislead those who are not familiar with macaw eggs into believing that they are infertile. The shape and size of eggs laid by different females of the same species can vary considerably. There can also be noticeable variation within the eggs from one clutch. If asked which species of parrot laid the largest egg, most people would unhesitatingly reply: the Hyacinthine Macaw. However, from the limited data I have collected, it would seem that Buffon's lay larger eggs, averaging about 54 × 42 mm (2 × $1^3/_5$ in.), while Hyacinthine eggs average about 49 × 38 mm ($1^4/_5$ × 1½ in.). The smallest macaw egg is that of the Hahn's, which averages about 31 × 25 mm ($1^1/_5$ × $^9/_{10}$ in.).

Incubation periods can vary according to climatic conditions. Eggs placed in an incubator from the time they are laid should hatch in the shortest time as they are incubated under optimum conditions, as should eggs incubated by the parents in a hot climate. For example, in Europe, the incubation period of the Blue and Yellow Macaw is usually found to be 26 or even 28 days, but in Gran Canaria, where the average daytime temperature is about 29°C (84°F), I have found that the eggs hatch after 24 days.

The incubation period is shortest in the small *Ara* species – a minimum of 23 days – and longest in the Hyacinthine, in which the minimum period is probably 27–29 days.

Fostering chicks

Occasionally one comes across a macaw which breaks eggs, but at the outset one must distinguish between accidental breakage of eggs with thin shells caused by a calcium-deficient diet, and purposeful breakage. Examine the remains of the egg; if it is thin-shelled, immediately start to give a liquid calcium and vitamin D_3 preparation in the drinking water or in bread and milk or another soft food. You can obtain calcium supplements from a veterinarian.

If the shell is good, try to break the habit at the outset. Empty an infertile egg and fill it with an unpleasant-tasting substance such as mustard, or substitute the real eggs with plastic eggs, usually made for pigeon fanciers and available at some large vendors of pet supplies. The real eggs can be placed in an incubator and returned to the nest when the chicks start to pip, or they can be placed with foster parents.

There is a degree of risk as this situation is totally unpredictable. Some birds will feed chicks of entirely different species, provided that they are about the same size or age as their own young; others will not even foster young of the same species. I would recommend that any breeder of large macaws keep a few pairs of small macaws or *Aratinga* conures as foster parents, as rearing macaw chicks from the egg is not easy. Willing foster

Two eggs (left) of the Hyacinthine Macaw (39 × 50 mm and 38·5 × 50 mm, respectively). On the right is an Illiger's egg (29·5 × 37·5 mm)

parents will do a much better job than you can for the first two or three weeks.

I shall discuss the subject in some detail because inexperienced pairs of macaws quite often fail to feed their first chicks; there can be nothing more frustrating for the new breeder, after the joy of seeing newly hatched chicks, than finding them unfed after one or two days.

At Loro Parque I often used a pair of Sun Conures (*Aratinga solstitialis*) to rear newly hatched macaw chicks. This particular conure female laid small clutches of only two eggs, only one of which would ever hatch. I could give her a newly hatched chick of any macaw species before or after her own chick hatched. On the first occasion, in desperation at watching a Blue and Yellow Macaw reared from the egg becoming thinner, I gave her a 13-day-old chick which weighed a pathetic 39 g ($1^3/_5$ oz). Seven days later it weighed 88 g (3 oz) and when removed from the nest, aged 28 days, it was a strong and healthy 209 g (7 oz). On one occasion this pair accepted a newly hatched Scarlet Macaw which was removed ten days later and replaced by a Military Macaw. This was also removed, at the age of two weeks, for hand-rearing.

Aratinga conures should not be expected to feed more than one young macaw of a large species for more than seven days: they could cope with two up to this age and then one would have to be removed. On one occasion a pair of Mitred Conures (*Aratinga mitrata*) fed two Blue and Yellow Macaws for this period before I removed one.

Many macaws are wonderful parents, and rear their young without any problems. However, one must be prepared for any eventuality or chicks could be lost when an emergency arises.

Even where the nest box design theoretically allows inspection of the nest, the larger macaws are often so protective of the nest that they refuse to leave when they have eggs or young. They will lunge towards the inspection door when it is opened and can be so aggressive that it is impossible to obtain more than a fleeting glimpse inside. Nevertheless, an attempt should be made to do so every day, especially with pairs which have not previously hatched chicks. If it is necessary to remove a chick, try to maneuver the parents behind the chicks and place a catching net between the chicks and the parents. This operation is often easier with two people, the task of one being to keep the macaws at bay and of the other to remove the chick as quickly as possible.

Not many breeders realize that parrots sometimes become impatient and begin to help a chick

A Blue and Yellow Macaw aged 46 days. It was reared by Sun Conures from the age of 13 to 28 days. It had been hand-fed from hatching, but fared very badly and weighed only 39g ($1^3/_5$oz) at 13 days. After 15 days with Sun Conures, it weighed 209 g ($7^3/_{10}$ oz)

Military Macaws

The Military
Macaw – a
somewhat
neglected
avicultural subject
until the late 1980s

A one-year-old
Military Macaw
reared at Loro
Parque, Tenerife

This Military
Macaw would
"blush" crimson at
the slightest
provocation

Parent-reared
Military Macaw
aged 34 days. Note
that it was fitted
with a 16-mm
band; the correct
size is 14 mm

Cap for a damaged egg of an Illiger's Macaw

Hibitane, cut it to fit over the surviving part of the shell and, after moistening the membrane with a little warm distilled water, I closed the egg with the new piece of shell, and placed it in an incubator. I was confident that the chick would survive. Next day I removed the shell several times to moisten the membrane again with distilled water. By the afternoon, the chick was calling loudly. By 7 a.m. next morning I was delighted to find that it had kicked off the borrowed shell and was in the

The Illiger's chick hatching from the damaged egg

out of the egg. In some cases this may be warranted, if the chick is in trouble. However, the most extraordinary case of egg opening that I have witnessed related to an Illiger's Macaw. She was an inexperienced parent. Her first chick died at one day old and she quickly nested again. Three eggs were laid, the first two of which hatched without incident on June 23. When checking the nest on June 27, I found that the female (presumably) had removed the entire top of the shell of the third egg, that is, all the shell had been removed that should have been covering the air space. I was shocked to see the naked embryo, covered in blood and wood shavings. Disastrous as it looked, I knew instinctively that the chick was alive, and quickly set to work with Q-tips and a warm solution of Hibitane disinfectant.

Having removed the wood shavings, I could see the embryo moving beneath what was left of the membrane, and also that hemorrhaging of the membrane was slight and could probably be tolerated by a chick which appeared to be two days away from hatching. Fortunately I had removed the hatched shells discarded by the previous two chicks (partly because an empty shell could become lodged over an unhatched egg, preventing it from hatching, and partly because shells in good condition can be very useful). I had stored the shells carefully.

I cleaned a shell in a solution of

process of "hatching."

I fed it a couple of times with a warm solution of Ringer's lactate, while deciding whether to place it in the nest of the parents. Would it be accepted? I recalled a similar incident when a chick from the damaged egg of a Hahn's Macaw was placed in the nest after being hatched in an incubator. It was immediately killed by its parents. I wanted this to be a success story. In the incubator I warmed an egg which was of a similar shape and size to that of the Illiger's, and placed it in the nest under the other two small chicks. My intention was to place the newly hatched chick in the nest in the shell, as parrots are more likely to accept chicks which hatch in the nest, rather than those which are introduced as chicks. However, this plan was thwarted by the nonacceptance of the egg by the parents. A couple of hours later I found it kicked to one side.

I did not want to rear the new

chick from the egg and therefore decided to remove the eldest chick for hand-rearing and replace it with the newly hatched chick. A check on the nest a few hours later revealed that the newcomer had food in its crop. All was well!

Rearing foods and calcium
If the young are left with the parents for the entire rearing period, few problems are likely to occur with experienced parents provided they accept a good variety of foods. It is vitally important to

A newly hatched Illiger's chick, weighing 11 g

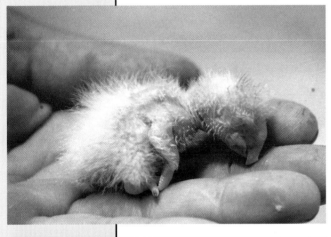

Illiger's Macaw aged 13 days

because it is so easy to prevent. Many macaws will consume bread and milk during the rearing period, and a liquid or powdered calcium supplement, or calcium carbonate, can be added to this. Cuttlefish bones and mineral blocks are good, but the larger macaws destroy them so quickly that they need to be replaced almost daily.

One can also make up a rearing food from any nutritious items on hand, as the larger macaws especially enjoy a mixture of cooked foods. For example, Dr. and Mrs. Nathan Gale in the United States made up a rearing food for their macaws consisting of four cups of cooked chicken scratch and four cups of rice, cooked in eight cups of water for about 45 minutes. To this was added 450 g (16 oz) of sweetcorn, 450 g of frozen mixed vegetables, six cups of parrot mixture, two heaped tablespoonfuls of vitamins and ¼ cup of dark Karo syrup. Four cups of dog food or monkey chow were added occasionally, plus brewer's yeast, bone meal and cod liver oil. This quantity lasted ten macaws three or four days.

At Palmitos Park all parrots receive daily a soft-food mixture of a crumbly consistency, made up of whole-grain bread, hard-boiled egg, grated carrot and low-fat cheese. Those with young are given an extra portion in the morning, and in the afternoon they receive the same mixture to which has been added more bread and Nekton lory mixture.

Illiger's Macaw aged 15 days

ensure that a good source of calcium, plus either vitamin D₃ or sunlight, is available. Chicks of large species have a proportionally greater need for calcium during the growing period; without it the bones will be soft, i.e., the young birds will be suffering from rickets, which may affect their wings and legs so seriously that there is no option but to put them down. Rickets in young birds is a tragedy

Buffon's Macaw

Buffon's Macaw at
Palmitos Park
breeding center

Buffon's is sometimes confused with the Military Macaw – but it is substantially larger, its plumage is a yellow shade of green and the tone of red in the tail is lighter

The first Buffon's reared in the United Kingdom and possibly in the world (at Paradise Park, Cornwall) seen here at about eight weeks old

During the rearing period, additional green food should be provided for those macaws that enjoy it. If possible, food should be provided three or four times daily to stimulate the parents to feed their young. Fresh corn on the cob should be offered twice daily, or even more often when available.

One problem which occasionally arises is plucking of the young by the parents. This is not serious unless flight feathers are removed, rendering the young unable to fly, or unless they are so badly denuded that they would be likely to die from cold when they left the nest. In such cases hand-rearing or fostering would be necessary. Otherwise the breeder's proudest moment comes when he or she sees young birds leave the nest. At first they will probably cling to the wire of the cage or aviary and will return to the nest after a short period, perhaps not emerging again for two or three days. Soon they will be confident enough to perch alongside their parents and copy all their actions. Small macaws will be independent of their parents, that is, feeding well on their own, after about three weeks, but should be left in the aviary for a couple of weeks longer. Large macaws should remain with one or both parents (should one behave aggressively it may be necessary to remove it until the young are independent, but this is not very likely) for at least five weeks, preferably a little longer provided that the parents are not becoming irritable at their presence. If the young remain with the parents too long, it will prevent them from nesting again in most cases.

Breeding macaws provides an enormous sense of satisfaction and personal pride. There is pleasure in observing their family life as well as in the knowledge that you are helping to ensure the future of macaws in aviculture.

As yet the potential breeding life of macaws is unknown. I believe that it could be as long as 35 or 40 years for the large species (possibly even longer) and 20 to 25 years for the small species. Given the prolificacy of some species, it can be seen that very large numbers could be and probably will be bred in captivity. No one can deny the significance of this in the conservation of macaws. Undoubtedly the day will come when there are more macaws in aviaries than there are in the wild. This will be a sad day, but through aviculture the macaws will be given a chance to survive. For hundreds of other bird species, this will not be the case.

BAND SIZES

	mm		mm
Hyacinthine	16	Red-fronted	12
Blue and Yellow	14	Severe	10
Blue-throated (Caninde)	14	Illiger's	9·5
Scarlet	14	Yellow-collared	9·5
Green-winged	16	Red-bellied	9·5
Military	14	Hahn's	7·5
Buffon's	16	Noble	8

If banding is left too late for the correct sized band, one which is 1 mm larger than recommended can safely be used in the case of the small macaws. In the large macaws, where the next size will be 2 mm larger, this might cause a problem. For example, a 16-mm band on a Blue-throated Macaw caused a callus on the leg.

8
Hand-rearing

There is a growing trend among parrot keepers towards removing all eggs of the larger and expensive parrots, hatching them in an incubator and rearing all the young by hand. I am adamantly against this. Hand-rearing is an invaluable method of increasing production and of saving chicks that cannot be reared by the parents, but it should not be a method which excludes all others.

If a clutch of eggs is removed from a macaw, she will generally lay again within three or four weeks. In this way, three or four or even more clutches could be obtained in a year. It is evident that, with birds as expensive as the large macaws, the financial rewards from a prolific pair could be great indeed. The temptation to turn such birds into egg-laying machines which never have a chance to rear their own young is too great for many breeders. I wonder if they have ever considered the psychological effect that the removal of eggs and unweaned chicks has on their birds. Most are deeply disturbed by this. No one yet knows what the long-term effect of never allowing macaws to rear their young will be, or how generations of incubator-hatched chicks will compare with those reared by their parents. However, aviculturists are surely heading for many breeding problems in the future if this practice is continued indefinitely.

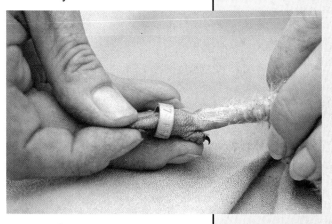

I would recommend that all macaws be allowed to rear one clutch of young per year, or at least every other year, provided, of course, that they care for the chicks well. Upon removal from the aviary the young will become tame in a few weeks if housed in a cage in close proximity to people.

The temperament of hand-reared birds depends on the species, the individual bird and the person rearing it. The personality of the sweetest macaw can, of course, be spoilt by an unsympathetic person feeding or handling it. Therefore hand-rearing in itself cannot guarantee the production of a macaw which is very tame and easy to handle.

The band is pushed over the front two toes and the outer back toe, then up the foot. The fourth toe may have to be released with a pointed matchstick when banding small species of macaws

Age of chicks when removed from the nest
Before you remove your first macaw chick for hand-rearing, remember that you must be highly committed to make a success of this long and demanding task. Do

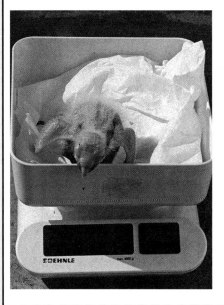

Digital electronic scales are recommended for daily weighing of chicks (such as this Illiger's) being hand-reared

not imagine that you can remove chicks just before they are due to leave the nest. At this stage they are very difficult to handle and will have to be force-fed at first. The ideal time to remove chicks is between two and four weeks, when they will be plump and well developed.

Rearing from the egg is not recommended unless you have plenty of experience in hand-rearing. The reason is that chicks which have never been fed by their parents, or other parrots, do not grow as well initially as those which are parent-reared. No matter how good the diet, it cannot reproduce the digestive enzymes which the parent passes to its chick. These are so powerful that chicks can even digest huge cropfuls of hard food at an early age. If you gave the same food to a hand-reared bird its crop would become compacted.

Hand-rearing is a complex subject – and only the basics can be covered here. (The subject is covered in detail in *Hand-rearing Parrots and other Birds* by Rosemary Low, published by Sterling, 1987.) The first essential for young chicks is a brooder or some other reliable heat source such as a heat pad. An aquarium makes an excellent brooder because it is easy to keep clean and allows you to view the chicks at all times. It needs to be fitted with a roof of wood or metal which holds two light bulbs controlled by a thermostat. This system gives the most accurate temperature control; alternatively, a room dimmer can be wired up to the light bulbs. This is satisfactory provided that the temperature in the room is not likely to fluctuate greatly.

Small chicks can be placed in plastic containers, which should not be shallow or large. Paper towel or tissues can be packed around them for the first few days. Although widely used, this material has the disadvantage that the bleach in the paper can cause minute cuts to the chicks' feet or wings, resulting in bleeding. Should this occur, a different material must be used,

such as a towel or face cloth.

After they are ten to 14 days old, small-mesh welded wire netting is the best surface for parrot chicks; it prevents foot problems and also prevents the chicks from swallowing wood shavings. Shavings or newspaper can be placed under the welded mesh; it will need to be changed once or twice daily.

Macaw chicks will soon outgrow a small container and can then be allowed freedom within the brooder. All the chicks from one clutch are best kept together, so a larger brooder may be necessary or, in warm conditions, they can be moved to a cage when they start to feather or to two large plastic laundry baskets, one inverted on top of the other to form a cage. The chicks can see out but the laundry basket provides a good degree of darkness and seclusion.

Feeding implements and methods

A syringe is the usual implement for feeding macaws; disposable plastic medical syringes are stocked by most pharmacies. However, I prefer bulb syringes, finding them easier to operate with one hand. I also prefer spoon-feeding to syringe-feeding because it is much safer (there is no danger of food entering the lungs as can occur when a syringe is used). It is also more natural as the chick feeds with a normal pumping action and ceases to feed when it has had enough. If the food is too hot or too cool it will be rejected from a spoon, whereas with a syringe the food is forced into the chick and it has no opportunity to reject food it does not want or to control the quantity it takes at one time.

It is very rarely that a spoon is used for feeding large macaws throughout the entire rearing period because spoon-feeding is more time-consuming than syringe-feeding. When rearing a number of chicks which have reached the stage where the volume of food being consumed makes spoon-feeding too time-consuming, I use a bulb

A dessertspoon with the sides bent inwards is the author's favorite instrument for hand-feeding. Syringes are more widely used for macaws

syringe, changing back to the spoon as the chick approaches weaning, when it wants to taste the food. At this stage it will nibble at small particles in the food which is now ground up less finely.

With a syringe, food can be placed in the mouth near the back of the tongue, or, by using a plastic tube on the end of the syringe, it can be directed into the crop. This is force-feeding and should be practiced only out of necessity, in my opinion. If a chick ceases to feed because it is sick or stressed, however, or if a young macaw has to be removed from the nest when it is fully feathered and impossible to spoon-feed, there may be no option but to force-feed for a few days.

Unless long-practiced in the task, this is best accomplished by two people. One holds the bird steady and also holds the top of the plastic tube on the end of the syringe. The force of the pumping action of a macaw can result in the plastic tubing losing contact with the syringe and the macaw could easily swallow the tubing. When filled, the syringe should be turned upside down and depressed a little to dispel any air. The second person then inserts the tubing into the *right* side of the bird's mouth and down the throat into the crop. The syringe is depressed slowly to release the food. The leading edge of the inner part of the syringe should be lubricated with petroleum jelly because

It is easy to observe how much food is in the crop. This chick's crop is empty. It is advisable to wait until the chick's crop is empty before feeding

The same chick five minutes later, after being fed. After feeding, be sure to clean the areas at the top of the throat and under the chin

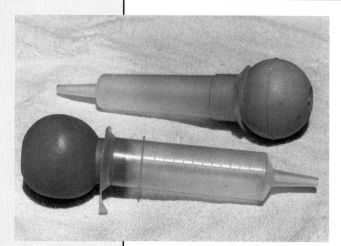

Bulb irrigation syringes are very useful for hand-feeding large macaws

Using a bulb syringe to feed a Hyacinthine

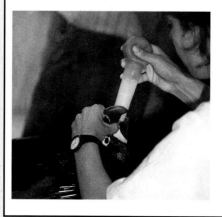

food have been used to rear macaw chicks. A few years ago these were mostly based on cereals and vegetables. Then, in the United States, it became fashionable to use monkey chow (even to the exclusion of all other foods) and now there is a trend towards using a commercially prepared formula. "Fast foods" are popular because they are time- and labor-saving, but I like to know exactly what I am feeding to my chicks, and the precise ingredients of these foods are not known.

The dietary requirements of macaw chicks which have been fed by their parents for three or four weeks are easily met, those from ten to 20 days may be a little more difficult and those under ten days need very careful attention. I have reared many species of parrots from the egg with a high success rate, but my highest failure rate has been with macaws and *Pionus* parrots. This does not necessarily mean that they are the hardest to rear; it could mean that the basic food I use is less suited to these two groups. I prefer to use foster parents for these chicks for the first ten to 14 days.

It is difficult to discover the success rate of other aviculturists in rearing chicks from the egg, since many are reluctant to disclose their failures. In the United States many breeders sell their macaw chicks before weaning and may not know how many of their young are reared to independence. However, this is not necessarily the most relevant statistic. If a chick has been incorrectly fed during the first few weeks of its life, vital organs, such as the liver and kidneys, may be affected but the bird could live for six months or more.

Many macaw chicks reared from the egg show a poor growth rate initially. In writing about this, I find it difficult to recommend a diet for newly hatched macaws since I tend to adjust the diet according to the response of the individual chick, whereas with lories, cockatoos, Eclectus Parrots, Gray Parrots, etc., there seems to be much less individual variation. The

syringe-feeding is difficult if the plunger does not move easily. The plastic tube should be dipped in warm water before being placed in the bird's mouth to ensure that it is not cold and slides easily into the crop. The food must be ground up very finely as the syringe will become blocked by small lumps. It is very frustrating to have to remove the syringe from the bird's crop in such a case and start all over again.

Syringes should be sterilized overnight in a solution of Milton or some similar product used for sterilizing a baby's bottle. Spoons are much easier to keep clean – another advantage. The only disadvantage is that if a spoon is used for several years it can wear down so much that it becomes sharp. For newly hatched chicks a teaspoon with the sides bent inwards can be used, the size of the spoon being increased as the chick grows.

Rearing food or formula
Countless different combinations of

reason may be that macaws have a higher requirement of protein in the diet and react more dramatically to a deficiency. They certainly need substantially more calcium than the smaller parrots (see Chapter 5).

Some successful diets, which have either been widely used or proved over a long period are as follows:

1 Purina monkey chow, usually with a small amount (10–20 percent) of fruit or vegetable baby food bought in jars, such as apple sauce or creamed corn.

2 Baby cereal, usually one of the vegetable range, and preferably mixed vegetable dinner, with a protein content of 16.7 percent wheat germ cereal or ground-up muesli, and sunflower seed kernels (obtained from a health food store) and ground finely.

3 At the Avicultural Institute, the well-known breeding station which formerly operated in California, 63 percent ZuPreem Primate Dry Diet (monkey chow, 20 percent protein content), 29 percent Roudybush Hand Feeding Diet, and 8 percent oatmeal. The monkey chow is ground into a coarse meal and blended with the other two items. This is added to warm water and then mixed with Gerber's baby food in jars (creamed corn, or oatmeal with banana and apple).

Obviously, water is added to all the mixtures described, the amount depending on the age of the chick. All these diets have been used for rearing *from the egg to weaning*.

Temperature and consistency of food
The consistency of food for newly hatched chicks must be very thin – thinner than milk. If you look at day-old parent-fed macaw chicks you will see that the crop appears to be filled with liquid. They cannot digest solid food. It is known that Budgerigars produce crop milk. No work has been

carried out on other parrot species with regard to this, but the same is likely to be true. If so, what stimulates its production? It cannot be a response to the end of the incubation period because one can foster newly hatched chicks (or pipping eggs) to a female whose own eggs are not due to hatch for a few days more, and they will be fed a very thin liquid.

The consistency of the food is gradually thickened. I prefer to use food which runs freely off the spoon until just before weaning, when it is thickened slightly. At this stage, and until weaning is completed, I give food similar to thin porridge – an imprecise description. The contents may be varied but a typical mixture would consist of the following: 100 g (3½ oz) of wheat germ cereal and 100 g of a mixed vegetable type baby cereal, plus blended fruit. The latter would consist of perhaps 300 g (10½ oz) of papaya, and 100 g of banana blended with 300 ml (10 fl oz) of water. Fruit and cereal are then mixed with about 800 ml (28 fl oz) of water and lightly cooked.

The temperature of the food needs to be highest for newly hatched chicks and lowest for those at the weaning stage. Hot food for young chicks should be tested by placing a drop on the back of your hand. As experience is gained, a thermometer can be used to test the temperature, and this should be placed in the part of the food container from which the food is to be taken. A microwave oven is not recommended for heating the food, as hot spots can develop. Many veterinarians have treated chicks which have had holes burned in their crops by overheated food – imagine the pain the chick must suffer! Spoon-fed chicks will shake their heads and refuse to swallow, or will spit out, food if it is too hot. Feathered macaw chicks will usually back away or even cry out. Most will take food that is only warm, whereas young chicks simply refuse to feed if offered warm rather than hot food.

Macaws preen their chicks after feeding them. Those being hand-reared will enjoy having their heads scratched instead. This also helps to remove the feather sheaths when they become dry and brittle. These would normally be removed by the parents

Care of the plumage

Macaws of all species have a very vigorous head-pumping movement when receiving food. This can result in food being spilled on the feathers at the side of the beak and under the beak. While making the head-pumping movements, macaw chicks simultaneously flick their wings. In some this is such a strong movement that it is almost impossible to prevent food from falling on the shoulders. The food must be wiped off the plumage immediately after feeding because it is difficult to remove once it has dried and causes stress to the chick. If food does stick, soak the feathers with warm water.

Parrots preen the plumage of their unfledged young to keep it in good condition and to remove the feather sheaths which enclose the growing feathers. These are removed from the head feathers, which the young birds cannot reach themselves. Sometimes, in hand-reared birds, probably because of lack of humidity, feather sheaths on the wings and tail become very hard, preventing the feathers from opening. In this case the sheaths can be removed by gently breaking or soaking them if they are hard and brittle.

After the age of about three months young macaws can be lightly sprayed with warm water to keep their plumage in good condition. This can become very dry in birds kept indoors. Spraying should be carried out only in a warm room indoors or on a sunny day out of doors.

Parrot chicks preen themselves from an early age – even before the feathers have erupted. Once the feathers do start to erupt there will be much debris from the sheaths in the bottom of the brooder.

Mention was made above of the wing-flicking behavior of young macaws being fed. This is still evident in some hand-reared macaws of a year or more. They often respond to the appearance of the person who reared them by giving a food-soliciting call and flicking their wings, although it may have been months since they were hand-fed.

If food sticks to the feathers of the throat, as it has with this Yellow-collared Macaw, the feathers should be soaked in warm water. Removal of the food is then easy

70

9
Weaning

Much good advice has been published in avicultural magazines on the subject of hand-rearing parrots, but very little has been written about weaning. One reason for this is that many very experienced breeders, especially in the United States, sell their young before they are weaned. They are therefore unaware of how much attention macaws require at the weaning stage, as, indeed, are many breeders who have hand-reared other parrots but not macaws.

At the time of writing I have hand-reared and weaned 84 species of parrots from 27 genera (including ten species of macaw); thus I am able to compare macaws at the weaning stage with other parrots. In my opinion macaws and cockatoos are by far the most demanding of the parrot family. One reason is that many become emotionally dependent on the person who feeds them, and breaking this dependency can be the most difficult part of the weaning process. At this point the detached observer will probably point out that this occurs because the person doing the rearing becomes too emotionally involved with his or her charges; yet some macaws have independent personalities and show no involvement at all with those caring for them.

Sometimes an extraordinary rapport exists between macaw and feeder – a deep bond which would be unlikely to occur with many other species of parrots. I have hand-reared hundreds of parrots, either from my own collection or in my capacity as curator at Loro Parque or Palmitos Park. Of all these, one will remain forever in my memory and etched on my heart – a male Blue-throated or Caninde Macaw which I reared in my apartment while at Loro Parque. For six months he and his sister ruled my life!

Anyone who has hand-reared many parrots cannot fail to notice the difference in temperament and personality in the various young. This is partly attributable to the species and also, especially in the larger parrots, due to individual personality and to sex. With the larger macaws, females are generally more docile and affectionate and males more independent and less demanding at the weaning stage. When a male and a female are reared together, the difference may be very noticeable. This is not always the case, however, and certainly did not apply with the two Blue-throated Macaws mentioned above. They were equally affectionate, docile and demanding.

Some people believe that weaning is the most difficult part of hand-rearing a macaw. This misconception arises because they fail to realize what a slow process weaning is, and they try to wean their young in four or five weeks, usually inviting disaster. The weaning process, that is, the period from when a young bird first eats solid food on its own, to the time when it is totally independent, lasts two or three months or even longer. Weaning may be lengthy but it is not difficult under normal circumstances.

Factors which affect the duration of the weaning period are the individual character of the bird, the age at which weaning is commenced, the foods offered, how many feedings are given from syringe or spoon and any traumatic events, such as being moved to a new location. The latter can set a young macaw back weeks, as it may entirely cease to feed on its own in strange surroundings and/or with people it does not know.

One of the finest weaning foods is fresh corn on the cob. This should be cut into lengths of about 5–8 cm (2–3 in.) and placed in the brooder with young macaws when they have about 50 to 70 percent of their feathers. This may be too soon; if the corn is left uneaten it can be given to another bird, but it is surprising how young some macaws are when they will start to nibble at corn and it is good that they should do so as early as possible.

When spoon-feeding, it is much easier to detect the signs that indicate that a young macaw wants to eat on its own. The bird will taste and chew the food, especially any particles, rather than swallow it. At the time macaws should start to feed on their own, they generally show more interest in flapping their wings or in playing than in feeding, when removed from the cage or brooder. When spoon-fed or syringe-fed into the mouth, a young parrot will make it very evident when it has had enough: it simply refuses to take any more food, or shakes its head and spits out the food. When syringe-fed into the crop, the bird has no choice but to accept the food.

One or two weeks after young parrots start to eat a little on their own, the quantity of food given by spoon or syringe can be reduced slightly, but I prefer to maintain the same number of feedings. Feeding by hand and giving slightly less than the birds are used to receiving stimulates them to nibble at the food in front of them. The most favored items, after corn, are generally soaked sunflower seed, peanuts in the shell, bread and plain crackers. Some also like banana, which should be cut up with the skin still in place.

Weaning foods
At this stage most macaws will relish a home-made soft food. Many combinations of ingredients can be used. An excellent example is that used by a friend, Sandra Mason, which consists of muesli soaked overnight in orange juice, crunchy peanut butter (the type with no salt or sugar added), small chunks of apple, grated carrot, a little grated cheese and mashed banana. This is blended with hot water to a soft consistency.

Young macaws do enjoy items that they can pick up; they may destroy more than they eat, but this is all part of the learning process. They may be given cracked walnuts, a large piece of carrot, large leaves of spinach or similar green vegetables, half a stick of celery, crunchy pieces of stale bread or rolls or pieces of toast. It may be some months before young *Ara* macaws are strong enough and adept enough to crack whole walnuts but they can be given halves at an early age.

Most young macaws enjoy grapes, oranges and bananas, but initially show more interest in carrots and other items that are hard and chewy than in soft fruits such as apple and papaya.

An alternative method
Some young macaws go through a stage where they will take only small amounts of food from spoon or syringe, yet are not eating sufficient on their own to sustain them. It usually helps to make the food more liquid as they will swallow this more readily than thicker food. Sometimes the key to the problem is to discover the consistency of the food, or the temperature, that the bird prefers. Often it will be found during this "difficult" period that there is one time of the day when more food will be taken, perhaps in the late afternoon, and that little is taken during the morning feedings. It is natural for any parrot to lose weight just before leaving the nest, so this is generally no more than a natural instinct to reduce food intake. Daily weighing will reveal whether weight loss is greater than normal. Usually this stage soon passes without too much cause for concern.

There is more than one way of weaning a macaw, and I have

Towards the end of the weaning period, some macaws will feed from a saucepan and thus spoon or syringe can be dispensed with

found that a method I use for weaning some lories can be successful with macaws which are slow to wean. I always feed with a spoon from a small saucepan used for heating the food. Birds which have been spoon-fed are easily encouraged to eat from the saucepan by filling the spoon from the saucepan but not moving it away from the surface of the liquid. Soon they will feed from the saucepan when it is set in front of them, and thus the spoon or syringe can be dispensed with. I weaned the two Blue-throated Macaws already referred to in this way. I would set two pans of food on the kitchen floor and call the birds. They would come running into the kitchen, almost falling over their feet in their haste, and gulp the food down.

When they are feeding well on their own, the number of feedings given daily can gradually be decreased until food is offered from syringe or spoon only twice daily, in the early morning and either the afternoon or evening, according to the needs of the young macaw. If, for example, three are raised from the same clutch, it is noticeable how each will differ in the amount of food taken from the hand-feeder; one may be independent a month before another and no attempt should be made to wean all three simultaneously if this development is evident. Each young macaw should be fed as long as is *necessary*. I emphasize the word

because occasionally one comes across a youngster who clings to the hand-feeding process as a means of maintaining its relationship with the feeder.

Cutting out one feeding daily and then both feedings and noting the daily weight loss or otherwise will indicate how necessary it is to continue to feed. If the bird genuinely needs feeding and it does not consume enough on its own, a drop in its weight will occur.

Macaws have a greater need to exercise their wings than any other young parrots. Few breeders will be able to keep them in cages large enough for adequate wing exercise to be obtained during the weaning period. For this reason, when let out for feeding, most macaws will vigorously flap their wings and, when older, will fly around the room. Most will make no attempt to feed until this important ritual has been accomplished. After a good flap comes a good feed!

Handling young macaws
Handling young macaws can be painful because their claws are sharp and strong. It is best to blunt claws with a nail file so that the birds can be handled in comfort. Handling can also be painful because some young ones bite. Sometimes this is out of fear, caused by rapid movements of the handler. Speak quietly and move slowly and the young ones will have more confidence.

Occasionally one comes across a malicious biter; such birds are very

Macaws, such as these Blue and Yellows, aged ten weeks, need to explore outside their cage as they reach the weaning stage. The bathroom is often a safe playground

unpleasant to handle. An attempt must be made to correct them by spreading the palm of one's hand in front of their face and saying "No!" decisively. Immediately return them to the cage; this is the greatest punishment that could be handed out and, with luck, they will soon get the message. On no account should a macaw be physically punished.

Many young macaws are lovable and affectionate in the extreme, and if they receive affection in return no problems will be experienced. Stroke their heads and talk quietly to them whenever they are removed from the cage. Problems may be experienced when macaws are reared in numbers, making individual attention virtually impossible. They will compete for the attention of the hand-feeder and may develop the habit of nipping.

Young macaws are extremely playful and inquisitive; they are naturally full of mischief and must be allowed to play and explore outside their cage. If they are returned immediately after they have been fed, they will protest by biting. When only one or two are being reared it is easy to give them a play period after they have been fed. Where there are a number this is very difficult but the problem can be solved by allowing them daily exercise in a large flight cage.

They should be given safe items to play with – fruit juice cartons, the cardboard roll from the middle of kitchen towel and small offcuts of untreated wood, for example.

Weaning cages
The correct accommodation for young macaws of the large species is very important before and during the weaning period. The age at which they will be removed from the heated brooder varies according to local climate, room temperature and species. I like to use what I describe as a weaning cage, as the transition from brooder to all-wire cage represents a big change in the environment of the young bird. If a weaning cage is not used, it is advisable to place the

This type of cage is suitable for chicks that no longer need heat and that are not yet perching

young macaw in a wire cage during the day for a few hours and return it to the brooder at night.

My weaning cages are, in effect, box cages, that is, only the front is made of welded mesh, the rest of the cage being constructed of an easily cleaned surface such as melamine or Formica. There is a removable tray of welded mesh on runners at least 2.5 cm (1 in.) above the floor, below which newspaper is placed. This cage is very easy to clean and disinfect and the newspaper is replaced twice daily. The welded mesh floor allows the droppings to fall through, ensuring the young are permanently on a clean surface, and also provides good exercise for the feet. No perches are used in the weaning cage. I prefer to house two young macaws together. The size of cage for two Blue and Yellow Macaws, for example, is 78 cm (31 in.) long, 50 cm (20 in.) deep and 60 cm (24 in.) high.

The next step is a cage constructed entirely of welded mesh in which the young macaws can perch and climb. For a single Blue and Yellow the recommended size is 61 cm (24 in.) wide and for two birds 91 cm (36 in.) wide. In both cases the cage should be 1 m (40 in.) high and 61 cm (24 in.) deep. The base is made of welded mesh and can either stand in a metal tray or simply have sheets of newspaper placed underneath.

A most important design feature

in a weaning cage or all-wire cage is the door. A *wide* door is essential for the large macaws, partly because they have an ungainly habit of stretching out their wings when handled, and partly because when they reach the stage of not wanting to return to their cage it is necessary to place them inside very quickly—an impossibility if the door is too small. It also makes them difficult to reach if they are reluctant to come out.

A wide door in one piece is too wide to operate easily. The door should be in two pieces, each about 25 cm (10 in.) wide, and will take up most of the front of the weaning cage. It is simply attached to the surrounding welded mesh by C-clips and the two sections can be held together by dog-lead clips or a padlock. Some young macaws learn to open dog-lead clips, depending on the type or regardless of the type!

In the weaning cage food is given on the floor. Water can be given in a spill-proof container if such a thing can be found and is not used as a toy. Water is not essential, as the liquid intake from the rearing food is still high. In the all-wire cage food and water should be placed at perch level, perhaps with another food container on the floor.

When a young macaw can perch comfortably it should be removed from the weaning cage. This is

A Hyacinthine Macaw, aged 51 days with a Blue and Yellow aged 44 days. It is better to rear two macaws of different species together rather than rear each bird alone

generally a few days before it would have left the nest, had it remained with its parents. A Blue and Yellow could be perching at 11 weeks and a small macaw at about seven and a half weeks.

There is usually no problem in housing different species of macaws together if they have been reared together. For example, I reared a Yellow-collared with a Blue and Yellow. During the weaning period the small macaw could be seen nestling under the wing of its large companion at night. I also reared a Hyacinthine with a Blue and Yellow. The main problem in this case was that the playful nature of the Blue and Yellow was in complete contrast to the solemn, almost superior Hyacinthine, which could never be persuaded to join in. It is far better to rear two single birds of different species together, rather than keep them alone. They will play, preen and squabble for hours; most important, competition for food is a spur to weaning. Also, a slightly younger bird will copy its more advanced companion and will thus be weaned earlier.

Understanding the young macaw
I believe that, of all the parrots, macaws and cockatoos are the most sensitive during the weaning stage. The gradual transition from spoon or syringe to becoming totally independent is only part of the weaning process. It can take much longer for them to become emotionally independent of the person who has fed them for so many weeks. In the wild the large macaws may spend as long as one year with their parents – and yet many breeders try to wean them at about 14 weeks. While many hand-fed macaws may be feeding almost totally on their own at this age (and others may be eight or nine months old before they are truly weaned), in aspects other than feeding they are still extremely immature.

Most large macaws show pronounced signs of immaturity until they are about 15 months old, when their temperament starts to change. They become much more independent and assertive and their formerly playful bites may become painful as they learn to exert more pressure with their powerful beaks.

Hand-reared macaws need the most careful attention when they are removed from their familiar surroundings after independence. It may disturb them so much that they revert to very immature behavior, take very little food on their own and will need to be hand-fed for a while. They are likely to react most adversely if several have been reared together and they are suddenly deprived of the companionship of the other macaws as well as that of the person or persons to whom they are most attached. Placing them with or near other macaws at this time often helps and encourages them to feed.

It often happens that the young macaw is removed to a new home where there are no other macaws. In this case, the new owner must spend a lot of time with the young macaw, talking to it and encouraging it to feed. Food dishes must be in an easily accessible position, preferably at the end of the perch it uses most.

Kindness and love
Young macaws are extremely sensitive creatures and must always be treated with kindness and love. Any wrong or unkind treatment by the person responsible for the bird will ruin his or her relationship with it for life. Macaws can bite very hard in fear or bewilderment; at all costs a violent reaction must be avoided.

An important factor to bear in mind is that macaws which have been hand-reared by one or more women may behave very aggressively when they first encounter men.

Private breeders should try to ensure that their young macaws are handled by both men and women throughout the rearing period.

The majority of people who breed macaws do not produce large numbers in commercial establishments but hand-feed perhaps three or four a year in their own home. Seldom do they have a room specially set aside for the purpose. Instead, the macaws will probably be brought up in the living room as members of the family. At the weaning stage young macaws have a tremendous need to explore, to climb and, above all, to flap their wings (large species). The smaller macaws pose no special problems, but a large macaw can wreak havoc in a house when it makes its first inept attempts at flight. Ornaments will fall and furniture will suffer – to say nothing of the condition of the carpets! The best place for practice flights and exploratory wanderings is, without doubt, the bathroom (with the toilet seat cover down), unless, of course, it happens to be carpeted. A tiled room with few obstacles and nothing of value which is breakable provides the answer and, if possible, young macaws should be allowed their freedom here twice a day. If they are permanently confined to cage or brooder they will be much more difficult to handle and troublesome to return. A good tip, regarding the latter problem, is to let them climb on the inside of the door, then swing the door shut.

A problem more likely to arise when macaws are reared in a domestic situation is jealousy. A young macaw can become so possessive of the person who feeds it that it will attack another member of the family who appears to be getting more attention, whether that member is a spouse, child, animal or another parrot. A Yellow-collared Macaw which was very active on the wing at the weaning stage was allowed to fly around while its companion, a Blue and Yellow, was being fed. However, at about 14 weeks it became so jealous and so demanding of my attention that it started to attack me while the larger macaw was being fed.

I have seen many other cases of jealous behavior in young macaws. The spouse or partner of the person to whom the macaw is most attached must take particular care. If the bird is destined for an outdoor aviary, or to be sold, the problem is only temporary, but if the idea is to keep the bird as a pet, it could have a serious effect on the harmony of the household. The only answer, if the bird is to be retained, is to place it in an aviary, indoors or out of doors, with a young bird of its own species so that, with luck, it will transfer its affections from an early age, or at least will mature in the company of its own species.

Treat as an individual
Some breeders expect their large *Ara* macaws which are hand-reared to be weaned at about 14 weeks. I have heard of Blue and Yellow Macaws being weaned this early, but wonder how the weaning is accomplished and whether they are truly independent. To me, independence means that a young parrot no longer wants or needs to take food from me. I never try to force the birds' weaning by limiting the amount of food from the spoon. This can mean that I am feeding them at least once a day until they are eight months old (rare cases) or it may mean that at 14 weeks they are taking two substantial feedings a day from me, while two weeks later they no longer wish to be fed. Every large macaw must be treated as an individual. This protracted weaning period does not occur in the small *Ara* species, most of which are weaned by four months.

It is detrimental to the development of large macaws to keep them in the house or hand-rearing room for the entire weaning period if they are slow to wean. Their need to exercise their wings cannot be fulfilled in such an environment. It is better to place them in an indoor or outdoor aviary and to continue to feed them once or twice a day. Most are extremely sensitive to the change of location and will not feed well for a few days. It may be necessary to increase the number of feedings temporarily, until they have adjusted to their new surroundings. It is best to place them in an aviary with other birds with which they have been reared or on their own – not with strange birds, of which they may be very much afraid. When large macaws at weaning stage are placed in an outdoor aviary they tend to behave like children who have been abandoned; they cry and fret and need constant visits from the person who has hand-reared them.

An important point to bear in mind about macaws which have just been weaned is that they eat far more than adults. The food may need to be renewed two or three times daily. Some breeders or owners may fail to realize what a large quantity of food these birds require.

In the United States the trend is to sell young macaws long before weaning age so that the new owner will accomplish the weaning. There are many disadvantages in this system (see Low, 1987). My advice would be not to embark on this unless you have an experienced hand-rearer of parrots in your vicinity, and also a good avian veterinarian.

WEANING WEIGHTS AND AGES OF SOME MACAWS

The ages at which hand-reared Macaws are weaned, that is, no longer dependent on being hand-fed, can vary from ten weeks to eight months, according to the species and depending on the individual bird. Below are some examples of weaning weights and ages.

SPECIES	AGE	WEIGHT g		BREEDER environment: p=private	z=commercial
Blue and Yellow	167 days	790	a*	p	
	141 days	770	a	p	
	148 days	840	a	p	
	173 days	880	b	p	
	175 days	910	b	p	
	110 days	range 700–1020 in 38 birds c			z
Blue-throated	8 months (at six months	610 female 586)	a	p	
	8 months (at six months	802 male 692)	a	p	
Scarlet	106 days	range 784–1027 in 9 birds	a		z
	105–120 days	average 870 in 8 birds	b		z
Red-fronted	192 days	454	a	p	
	97 days	396–437 in 3 birds	b		z
Illiger's	66 days	230	a		z
	about 97 days	221	b		z
	about 97 days	234	b		z
Yellow-collared	105 days	n/a	a	p	
	95	210	b	p	
Hahn's Macaw	about 70 days	116	a		z
Spix's	about 70 days	410	a	p	
	about 70 days	333	a	p	

a, b and c are used to denote different breeders for the same species

10
Genus *Anodorhynchus*

The three blue macaws which comprise this genus are basically similar, differing in size and shade of blue only. It has even been suggested that they should be considered conspecific (subspecies of one species, rather than different species). They differ from *Ara* macaws in lacking bare cheeks (or partly bare, decorated with lines of feathers), instead having a semicircular area of bare yellow skin at the side of the lower mandible. The bare skin surrounding the eye is also yellow.

HYACINTHINE (HYACINTH) MACAW
Anodorhynchus hyacinthinus
(Color pages 18/19)

Derivation: *Anodorhynchus* is from the Greek: *an* (without), *odous* (tooth) and *rhynchos* (beak), meaning beak without tooth, because, unlike macaws of other genera, the interior surface of the upper mandible lacks notches (ridges); *hyacinthinus* refers to the plumage, which is the color of a hyacinth.

Plumage: violet-blue, a deeper shade on the wings. The underside of the wings and tail feathers is blackish blue.

Length: approximately 100 cm (39 in.).

Weight: approximately 1,200 to 1,400 g (42–49 oz) but much wider ranges have been recorded.

Soft parts: there is a crescent-shaped area of yellow skin on either side of the lower mandible, a conspicuous area of yellow skin surrounding the eye and a line of yellow on the otherwise black tongue. The feet are gray.

Beak and eyes: the beak is black and the iris is dark brown.

Immature birds: differ from adults only in the shorter tail.

Captive status: uncommon and very highly priced. Appendix I of CITES.

Pet potential: it cannot be denied

A pair of Hyacinthine Macaws and their youngster (left) soon after fledging, reared at Loro Parque

that captive-bred, hand-reared birds, obtained when young, make wonderful pets for the few who have the money to purchase them, the time to devote to one of the most demanding pets it is possible to own, the space and finances to house such a powerful and destructive bird and the money to repair the damage to home or aviary! However, one has to consider the ethics of keeping a rare and endangered species as a pet and denying it the opportunity to breed. I believe that this bird should not be considered as a pet until far more are being reared in captivity. It must also be remembered that the voice of this species is extremely powerful and would be certain to annoy all but the most tolerant of neighbors with its screams.

Breeding: to date most successes have been achieved in the United States but the Hyacinthine Macaw is being bred in small numbers in all countries where aviculture is popular: the United Kingdom, Germany, the Netherlands, Sweden, etc.

This species has reared young under a variety of circumstances, from small indoor enclosures to large outdoor aviaries.

The normal clutch size is two; rarely, three eggs are laid. Even rarer, on a single occasion, a four-egg clutch has been recorded in the United States. The interval between eggs is usually three days but can be up to seven days. Incubation periods of between 27 and 32 days have been recorded but the norm seems to be 28 or 29. Newly hatched chicks weigh between 19 and 25 g. Some breeders have found that if two chicks hatch, only one will be fed after a few days, so a close watch on the development of a second chick is essential. Banding should be carried out at about four weeks with 16-mm bands. Young leave the nest at about 97 days. There are few data on parent-reared young but in the case of a pair owned by Pamela Bompart of Montana, after they leave the nest, the male feeds them – but not enough – so they then have to be removed for hand-rearing. They are very docile and easy to tame but are not fully independent until the age of five months.

In 1989 a pair at Palmitos Park, which had had eggs on several previous occasions, produced two infertile eggs at the beginning of May. These were removed after two weeks.

The female laid two more eggs, almost certainly on July 26 and 29. Chicks hatched in the nest on

Hyacinthine
Macaw

August 22 and 25, to give an incubation period of 27 days. In both cases the first pip mark was made 48 hours before hatching but there was no further progress for about 40 hours.

The day after hatching, the first chick weighed 26 g with about 3 g of liquid food in its crop. On hatching, the second chick weighed 25 g. The chicks were weighed every morning about 9 a.m. when their crops were full, and the following weights in grams were recorded:

Raspberries and cream are not exactly recommended – but they will do no harm once in a while

Day	Chick	
	No 1	No 2
hatch	–	25
1	26	28
2	34	32
3	38 (empty crop)	40
4	46	52
5	51	59
6	66	72
7	80	88
8	88	104
9	106	120
10	122	130
11	132	162
12	154	182
13	166	198
14	186	230
15	222	250
16	248	280
17	270	302
18	282	330
19	320	358
20	336	396

I hand-reared the chicks from the ages of 28 and 31 days. Their parents had fed them mainly on fresh corn, sprouted sunflower seed, walnuts, tomatoes and oranges.

Dietary preferences of the adults may alter considerably while they are rearing young. In the United Kingdom this species was first bred in 1983 by Daphne and Walter Grunebaum. Soon after this pair hatched their chicks they started to search for grit and consumed much ground-up limestone and cuttlefish bone. Their diet included Brazil nuts, walnuts and peanuts, sunflower seed, sweet corn, carrots, bananas, apples, grapes, peas and broad beans. When their first chick was six weeks old, the parents started to consume large quantities of hazelnuts, even in the green stage.

The area in which Mrs. Grunebaum resides is a rural one, and she allows the pair to fly at liberty for part of the day, weather conditions permitting. On one occasion I witnessed the pair flying while there was a chick in the nest. I was also privileged to share my raspberries and cream with Woggy, the first youngster reared by the pair. He was found on the aviary floor in a very weak condition after leaving the nest and had to be taken into the Grunebaums' 200-year-old cottage to be nursed to recovery. There he has resided ever since, enchanting all comers with his beauty, personality and talking ability. A tame Hyacinthine can be the most gentle creature imaginable. It could sever your finger as if it were a toothpick, yet is docile and doglike in its devotion to its human friends. However, I also recall one which was hand-reared at Loro Parque. On a couple of occasions before it was weaned, it took my wrist in its huge beak and clamped its mandibles together. This was carried out in an exploratory manner, with no hint of maliciousness. Nevertheless, it hurt, and gave me a taste of the

Red-fronted Macaws

Red-fronted and larger macaws can open whole walnuts; they must be cracked for smaller species

Five young Red-fronted Macaws bred in Florida by Richard Schubot

Severe Macaws

Perhaps because it is not brightly colored, the Severe Macaw attracted little attention from aviculturists until the late 1980s

This is the form of the Severe Macaw that has less blue on head and breast

Although not described in the literature (according to which size is the most relevant factor in distinguishing the subspecies), there appear to be two plumage forms. That shown here is bluer on the head and breast

A Hyacinthine Macaw, aged 72 days, hatched at Loro Parque and reared with a Blue and Yellow Macaw

punishment a Hyacinthine could administer if it so wished.

This particular macaw was hatched by a Blue and Yellow and reared with three chicks of that species until the age of about four weeks when it was removed along with one of the *ararauna* chicks. The personality of a Hyacinthine chick is as different from that of an *Ara* as that of an Amazon, for example. One has to exercise care in weaning Hyacinthines and not spoil them with too many nuts, or they may later refuse sunflower seed.

Hyacinthine Macaws reach sexual maturity at four to five years. I would strongly urge anyone keeping a single bird as a pet to find a mate for it before it reaches this age. The rewards of owning a pair and eventually obtaining breeding success are far greater in terms of achievement and in the personal satisfaction that comes from being a producer, not a consumer, of a rare species.

Origin: Brazil, south of the Amazon, also extreme eastern Bolivia in the department of Santa Cruz. It also occurs in extreme northeastern Paraguay, where it is almost extinct. Its range in Brazil has contracted very seriously in recent years.

There is seasonal movement of birds into Bolivia and perhaps also into Paraguay.

Natural history: trapping for the live bird trade has probably done more harm to this species than any other parrot in the neotropics, except, of course, Spix's Macaw. During the 1970s the volume of trade became so great that at one stage the market was saturated. The number of people able to look after these large and demanding birds satisfactorily is very limited; thus the degree of wastage must have been appalling. I remember when prices fell very low and dealers could not sell all the Hyacinthines they had stocked. Intensive trapping was occurring in the pantanal region of Brazil, and then birds would be smuggled across the Bolivian border and exported from Santa Cruz or sent down the Paraguay River to Asunçion in Paraguay because export from Brazil was illegal. The numbers exported from these two countries could not possibly have originated there. Then trade diminished and prices rose again. In 1987, the Hyacinthine was placed on Appendix I of CITES; this, if anything, had the opposite effect to that desired. Hundreds of birds were exported illegally, many of them to dealers in Paraguay, to find a ready market in many countries throughout the world.

No one knows how many Hyacinthines existed prior to the 1970s when the export trade in this species was very small, although local trapping occurred, often for food. In 1987 Charles Munn, Jørgen Thomsen and Carlos Yamashita (on behalf of CITES Secretariat) estimated the total population at between 2,500 and 5,000, optimistically, but felt the total was nearer to 3,000. At least the latter number must have been exported in that and the previous decade. At a conservative estimate, at least five die for every one exported, so it is not difficult to imagine the toll that trade has taken on this magnificent macaw. There are two reasons why the numbers captured have been so high: first, the obvious beauty of the bird and the high price it demands, and second, the fact that it is so easy to trap. Unlike *Ara* macaws, which are very wary, Hyacinthines will literally walk into a trap and are almost naturally tame.

Only in remote areas have substantial population declines not occurred. In some areas the Hyacinthine is still fairly common; in others it has gone forever. The favored habitat is not rain forest but gallery forest in semiopen areas, deciduous woodland, dry woodland savanna (cerrado) and buriti palm (*Mauritia flexuosa*)

swamps. Degradation of habitat, especially the removal of large trees suitable for nesting, is probably another important factor in the decline of the Hyacinthine Macaw. However, in some parts of its range, this species nests in cliff faces.

The diet appears to consist entirely of hard nuts and the fruits of various species of palms.

Conservation: even when the illegal export trade finally ceases, which will surely be soon (at the time of writing Argentinian exporters were finding it impossible to obtain customers because they could not provide CITES papers), pressure on the population of this macaw will not cease. Within Brazil it will continue to be hunted for food and for plumage, and its habitat will continue to be reduced, year by year, and its nest trees destroyed. It is inevitable that the captive population of the Hyacinthine Macaw will become increasingly important and may eventually be the means of keeping the species extant.

Aviculturists, then, must look on their role as that of guardian where this most magnificent of macaws is concerned. Not only must they

Two Hyacinthine Macaws, aged 17 weeks, reared by the author at Palmitos Park

Illiger's Macaw (1)

Illiger's Macaw aged 23 days and, below, the same chick 11 days later, at Palmitos Park breeding center

Illiger's is the only small macaw whose population is known to have suffered a serious decline. In October 1989 this species was placed on Appendix I of CITES

make every effort to breed from the birds in their care, but also they must ensure that when they part with the young they do so in a responsible manner. Because of the extreme docility of this species and the lovable temperament of hand-reared birds, almost all young in the United States are sold as pets, having been hand-reared. The latter practice guarantees tame young and, of course, increased production. However, what will be the effect of generations of hand-reared birds? As yet we do not know. It surely makes sense to allow pairs to rear their young on occasions, even if only once in every two years. It is, in my opinion, important that all macaws, but especially Hyacinthines because of the role that the captive population will ultimately play, be permitted to rear their young from hatching to weaning, on occasions.

LEAR'S MACAW
Anodorhynchus leari
(Color page 22)

Derivation: the species is named after Edward Lear (1812–88), the artist (famous for his nonsense poems and for such works as *Illustrations of the Family of Psittacidae, or Parrots*).

Plumage: entirely deep blue, almost the same shade as the Hyacinthine – but the depth and glossiness are slightly less intense. The plumage is a richer blue on the back, wings and upperside of the tail. The inner webs of the primaries, the under-wing coverts and the underside of the tail are blackish.

Length: about 75 cm (29 in.).

Weight: about 940 g (33 oz).

Soft parts: there is a semicircular area of bare skin adjoining the lower mandible, which is more extensive than in the Hyacinthine, and there is a small area of yellow skin surrounding the eye. The tongue is black with a yellow stripe on each side.

Beak and eyes: the beak is black and the iris of the eye is black.

Immature birds: do not differ in plumage. According to Ed Bish,

curator at Busch Gardens, Tampa (where several Lear's were reared), the bare skin surrounding the beak and eyes starts to color at about one year of age. Before then it is whitish. If it is normal for the skin to take this long to color, Lear's differs from the Hyacinthine in which the skin is pale yellow befor the chick is even fully feathered.

A Lear's Macaw hatched in July 1982 at Busch Gardens, Florida and hand-reared by Mr and Mrs Scherr at Parrot Jungle. The chick is seen here at two or three days old

Captive status: extremely rare and on a par with Spix's Macaw. Fewer than 20 worldwide.

Pet potential: it would be unthinkable to keep such a highly endangered species as a pet.

Breeding: regrettably, at the time of writing there are no reproducing pairs in captivity. The great scarcity of this species has meant that, until the early 1980s, when attempts were made to bring them together, captive birds had not been given the opportunity to breed. The first success was the result of cooperation (long overdue) between two well-known collections in Florida: Busch Gardens in Tampa and Parrot Jungle in Miami. The male of the breeding pair had been on exhibit for 27 years at Parrot Jungle before being sent to Busch Gardens. The pair were introduced on June 27, 1982, and within 60 days the female had laid; unfortunately, however, the three eggs were infertile. Two more infertile clutches, of three and two eggs, were laid. In the fourth clutch of two eggs, both hatched. One chick was removed from the nest at one day old and flown to Miami, where it was hand-reared by Mrs. N. Scherr, wife of the owner of Parrot Jungle. The second chick was left with the parents, but did not survive. In 1983 two chicks were hatched but, sadly, they both died. Two young hatched in 1984, on June 27 and 29, and are, at the time of writing, in the breeding center (off-exhibit) at Busch Gardens. One was hand-reared there and the other at Pet Farm, Miami, by Dr. Susan Clubb.

Because of the vulnerability of the small wild population, it is extremely important that Lear's Macaw should be established in aviculture, but there are so few birds to work with that this seems unlikely. The loss of the female of the breeding pair at Busch Gardens in 1988 was a tragedy. At about this time there were two females at Birdland, Bourton-on-the-Water in England, at least one of which had laid. One died and the other was offered for sale for £15,000. It is very sad when endangered species are in the hands of those who view them only in the light of how much cash they will realize, but it is especially disturbing when the individual bird concerned could play such an important role in the future of the species.

At the time of writing there are several specimens in a zoo in France, one in England, one in South Africa and probably five or six in Brazil. I saw three there in 1988, a magnificent bird in São Paulo Zoo and two unsexed Lear's in the collection of Nelson Kawall, also of São Paulo. One of these, an old bird, had been "repatriated" from Antwerp Zoo in Belgium.

Origin: the Bahia region of northeastern Brazil. The exact locality was discovered as recently as 1978, although Lear's Macaw has been known in captivity for well over a century. When the second edition of Forshaw's classic *Parrots of the World* was published in 1978, he stated of Lear's: "Exact range unknown, but probably north-eastern Brazil in the states of Pernambuco and Bahia." Of no other species of neotropical parrot did Forshaw state: "exact range unknown."

It was not the case that no one had ever tried to find the home of Lear's Macaw. Helmut Sick, the German-born ornithologist from Brazil, had been searching since 1964, but, given the size of the region and the impenetrability of much of it, the search was rather like looking for a needle in a haystack. In 1974 Sick was joined in his search by Dante Teixeira of the Museu Nacional, Rio de Janeiro. Sponsored by the Academia Brasileira de Ciencias, they searched tributaries of the Rio São Francisco in northwestern Bahia until 1976. They found only the Hyacinthine Macaw, which there, and in Piaui, reaches its easternmost limit.

On December 29, 1978, Sick and Texeira found the flight feathers of a blue macaw which had been shot for food. Two days later they encountered Lear's Macaw in the wild in the Raso da Catarina. They described this as an inhospitable area, very, very hot and lacking water. It was a plateau cut by canyons and dried-up river beds; there were no roads or settlements. Most of the area is covered with deep, loose sand and low, thorny vegetation (*caatinga*). It seemed an unlikely habitat for a macaw (Sick and Texeira, 1980).

In the following weeks, however, up to 21 Lear's were observed in a single flock. They fed on the small nuts of the licuri palm (*Coccus*) which they sometimes found by walking about on the ground. They also went on long flights in search of food.

Sick and Texeira recorded:

We reached roosting places of the macaws, situated in hollows in the upper part of the grotesquely eroded walls of the canyons. In such a place, where the birds arrive just before dusk, we counted up to 18 individuals.

Illiger's Macaw (2)

Illiger's Macaws at 13 and 17 days. Young grow rapidly and adult weight is attained at about 28 days

Illiger's Macaw at 27 days. This is the chick referred to on page 60 that nearly died in the egg when it was opened prematurely by the parents

Illiger's has proved itself exceptionally prolific in captivity. One pair reared 120 young by themselves between 1978 and 1989

Here we could study completely undisturbed, as they climbed on the vertical rock face and defended themselves against the flies swarming around them.

More recently, a Brazilian ornithologist has reported the presence of Lear's Macaw in an area outside the Raso da Catarina (withholding the location to protect the population there). This information gives new hope for the survival of this very rare macaw.

Natural history: Helmut Sick believed that the Raso da Catarina population numbered about one hundred, perhaps fewer.

Alexander Brandt located eight feeding places of this macaw in an area of 140 sq km (54 sq mi). Its food included the seeds of pinhao (*Jatropha pohliana*), the flowers of sisal (an agave) and ripening or dry corn. These macaws have been attacking corn for at least ten to 20 years, according to the local people. It takes one bird 20 minutes to eat a full ear of corn. The fruits of the palm trees are a favorite, but seasonal, food. For example, in July, when palm fruit availability is low, the macaws spent 26 percent of their time foraging on corn crops and only 6 percent in palm trees in the breeding area where observations were concentrated. The macaws spent 50 percent of their time resting and 36 percent feeding in palms. The largest number of Lear's seen during the study period was 58 in the roosting cliffs.

Conservation: land within its habitat was not expensive. Brandt suggested that areas within the breeding and roosting sites should be purchased.

Financial support should be provided for the farmers in view of the fact that their corn crops are eaten by the macaws. Cattle and goat grazing may prevent the recovery of palm stands; thus their re-establishment should be promoted by protecting small areas from grazing. Funds would be required for fencing such areas. When the palms reached a certain size, grazing could again be permitted. A small research station is needed. Personnel could plant corn and provide extra food.

Brandt concluded that the survival of this species is directly related to the attitude of the local people. To date there has been a "very positive response" from them. They provided Brandt with information on sightings and one landowner offered land in the main feeding area for research. Brandt feels there should be a local education program.

GLAUCOUS MACAW
Anodorhynchus glaucus

Derivation: *glaucus* is from the Greek *glakós*, meaning grayish green or blue.

Plumage: differs from that of Lear's only in the shade, which is more greenish blue. The tail is greenish blue above and the shaft of the feathers is brown. (After comparing two skins of Glaucous with one of Lear's, Glaucous appeared to me almost as a cinnamon mutation of the latter – although this could not be the case.) Glaucous has paler brown under-tail coverts and a brownish gray throat.

Length: 72 to 75 cm (28–29 in.).

Weight: unknown but probably about 900 g (32 oz).

Soft parts: the bare skin surrounding the eyes and at the base of the beak is yellow. In the two specimens I examined, the area of bare skin at the base of the beak was less extensive than in Lear's. The feet are blackish gray.

Beak and eyes: the beak is black. The width of the lower mandible in the two specimens examined was 50 mm ($1^9/_{10}$ in.) (compared with 45 mm (1¾ in.) Lear's). The iris is dark brown.

Immature birds: not described.

Captive status: assumed unknown at the time of writing. However, this extremely rare macaw has been held in captivity. One Glaucous lived in Buenos Aires Zoo in Argentina for over 20 years. It had been there that length of time when Sydney Porter (1938) saw it. At that time it was reputed to be over 45 years old. Porter commented: "Although its plumage was in very good condition the bird was evidently suffering from senile decay." Porter traveled widely and was extremely knowledgeable on the subject of parrots. This was the only Glaucous he had ever seen. London Zoo first exhibited this species in 1886; there was apparently a live Glaucous at the Jardin d'Acclimation in Paris from 1895 until 1905.

Origin: this species has not been officially recorded in the wild since the nineteenth century. It was known, or thought to occur, in southeastern Brazil, northeastern Argentina (Misiones and Corrientos), northwestern Uruguay (Artigas) and probably northern Paraguay.

Natural history: this macaw may or may not be extinct. The fact that it has not been observed in the wild for a century is not significant. It is easy to "lose" a species in the vastness of Brazil.

The first indication that this species is still extant came from the late Rossi dalla Riva, who lived in Brazil, and who kept, and on a few occasions bred, rare native parrots. He was extremely well informed about the status and origin of species in his area. In 1970 the Italian aviculturist Paolo Bertagnolio wrote to dalla Riva asking if there was any evidence of the existence of the Glaucous Macaw. On April 20, 1970, dalla Riva replied: ". . . it seems certain that the latter [Glaucous] nests in a locality not very far from here (a locality that, as in the case of *A. brasiliensis*, I prefer not to reveal otherwise local collectors would immediately send their hunters and trappers.)" (Bertagnolio, 1981).

He never did reveal the locality. It was over a decade later that I heard a rumor that two Glaucous Macaws had been taken to the United States. I dismissed it, assuming that the species concerned was Lear's. Then a well-known American bird collector indicated that he had been offered a nestling Hyacinthine Macaw in Bolivia, which he rejected because of its small size and dull color. Later it suddenly occurred to him that perhaps the poor creature was not a Hyacinthine! Could it be a Glaucous? He returned to discover that, alas, it had died. In 1988 a very experienced bird trapper spent some months in the field, completely out of contact with the outside world. He finally returned with the news that he had seen Glaucous Macaws but was unable to trap them to obtain photographic evidence.

Ridgely (1981) wrote: "Exactly what happened to the Glaucous Macaw is a mystery." Early observers, among them Azara (1805), found them quite common along the Parana River in the late eighteenth century; here he saw "a number of pairs" and noted that "it nested not only in hollows of trunks, but also, and with greater frequency, in ones made in the vertical banks of the Parana and Uruguay rivers."

It would appear that neither deforestation nor any other form of habitat disturbance can have caused its decline, for extensive forest remains over much of the species' former range, especially in Paraguay. Ridgely states that only in the last few decades, long after the decline of the Glaucous, did serious habitat disturbance begin to take place. He suggested that it was the first South American bird to become extinct since Western colonization.

Wild specimens were taken up to at least 1860 in Corrientes, Argentina, and can be seen in the United States National Museum in Washington.

Conservation: the "rediscovery" of the Glaucous would focus so much attention on it that its survival would immediately be threatened. With the best will in the world, the creation of a reserve and wardens to protect it, it would be nothing short of miraculous if someone did not find a way to trap some specimens. Very special precautions would have to be taken to ensure its survival.

Yellow-collared Macaws

Yellow-collared Macaws aged three, six and nine days. Note how quickly the beak color changes – it is different in each chick

The same Yellow-collared Macaws eight days later, aged 11, 14 and 17 days

Yellow-collared Macaw: hand-reared birds make wonderful pets, arguably the best of the small macaws

The Yellow-collared Macaw was unknown in aviculture until the early 1970s. It has proved very prolific

11
Genus *Cyanopsitta*

The single member of this genus is the most distinctive of all macaws, immediately distinguished by its pale shade of blue below and its grayish blue head. The cheeks are feathered, only the lores and a narrow area surrounding the eye being bare. The fact that the skin surrounding the eye is dark, not light, sets it apart from all other macaws.

SPIX'S MACAW
Cyanopsitta spixii (Color page 23)

Derivation: *cyano* is from the Greek *kyaneos*, meaning dark blue, *psitta*, meaning parrot is an abbreviated form of the Greek *psittakos*; *spixii*, named after Johannes Baptist von Spix (1781–1826), a German Doctor of Philosophy and of Medicine.

Plumage: it is a soft shade of cobalt-blue above, grayish blue on the head and neck and pale gray, rather than blue, on the head beneath the eyes. The underparts are paler blue than the upperparts. The underside of the tail is black, as are the inner webs of the primaries. The proportions of this macaw are more slender than those of any other.

Length: 55 cm (22 in.).

Weight: two adult birds have been weighed; the male was 389 g (13½ oz) and the female 332 g (11½ oz).

Soft parts: the bare skin of the cere and lores and surrounding the eye is dark gray; the feet are lighter gray.

Beak and eyes: the beak is black and proportionately smaller than in other macaws. The iris is pale yellow.

Immature birds: darker blue than adults, especially on the upperparts, with a shorter tail; the bare facial skin is light gray. The beak is dark gray with a broad white stripe down the culmen (middle of upper mandible). This stripe was still present in young bred by Antonio de Dios when they were aged 364 and 371 days, respectively.

Captive status: extremely rare. In October 1988 only seven were positively known outside Brazil and seven (or perhaps nine) in collections within Brazil. The existence of others was possible.

Breeding: at the time of writing, there are only two known adult pairs set up for breeding; the pair belonging to Antonio de Dios in the Philippines and the pair at Loro Parque, Tenerife. The latter were not old enough to breed until 1989, when a single egg was laid in May. The first overseas captive breeding occurred in the Philippines in 1988. I am indebted to Antonio de Dios for the following information.

The pair were obtained in late 1979. The birds had a choice of four nest sites: three trunks of buli palms and one nest box. They chose a small palm trunk which was hung horizontally. Two eggs were seen on May 29. When the nest was inspected on June 29 there were one chick and four eggs. By July 2 a second chick had hatched and the other eggs were discarded in one corner of the nest box.

The two chicks were removed for hand-rearing on July 15 when they weighed 255 g (9 oz) and 147 g (5 oz) with full crops. On July 27, aged 33 and 26 days, they weighed 334 and 224 g (11½ and 8 oz), respectively. On August 2, at 39 and 32 days, they weighed 390 and 273 g (13½ and 9½ oz), respectively; the eldest was fed 40 to 42 ml of food five times a day and the second was fed 30 to 32 ml. They were fed on a mixture made from one cup of pellets (soaked in water for ten minutes), half a cup of Roudybush Diet (obtainable

A male Spix's Macaw. Note the small beak of this species

mixture consisting of coconut, stringbeans, zucchini, cucumber, carrot, bell pepper, beef, eggs (scrambled in water), cheese, sweet potato, kidney beans, okra, papaya, plantain (similar to banana), guava or the native fruit of chico, mixed with calcium and vitamin additives. (This mixture was described as regular salad.) From the salad the carrots, okra and beans were preferred. The birds also liked the pellets: at weaning macaws always like crackers, pellets or anything else they can crumble up. These birds were then learning to fly and were transferred to a cage.

At 152 and 159 days they were still fed three times a day with 30 ml of food and were also eating bread, sprouted beans and boiled whole corn. By the end of January 1989 the amount of food was gradually decreased to 15 ml. The eldest started to pluck its feathers, so it was moved near a window. On July 6, 1989 (at 371 and 364 days), the young Spix's weighed 369 and 283 g (13 and 10 oz). Hand-feeding had ceased at the beginning of April.

In April 1989 the parents nested again. On April 14 the female stayed inside the nest all day. The male, which was becoming aggressive, entered only to feed the female. When the nest was inspected on May 15, five eggs were found. Four days later the female spent half the day out of the nest. Inspection revealed three stale eggs and two in which the embryos had died.

On June 6 the female was again spending all day in the nest. Inspection on June 15 revealed four eggs; two of these were placed in an incubator and one hatched.

The breeding pair is fed on the "regular salad" (described above), and a seed mixture including sunflower, daily at 7 a.m.; more salad plus sprouted mung beans, red, green, black and yellow, also green peas and cantaloupe is provided in the afternoon.

At 3.30 p.m. fresh corn on the cob is given, plus parrot pellets and two almonds and two hazelnuts per

from Roudybush, P.O. Box 331, Davis, Ca 95617–0331), and two tablespoonfuls each of the following Heinz baby foods: yellow vegetables, green vegetables and apple sauce. This was blended with 2½ cups of water for five minutes and then heated.

At 48 and 41 days the chicks weighed 400 and 300 g (14 and 10½ oz) and were fed 45 and 35 ml of food, respectively, five times a day. In both, the feathering on the wings was almost complete. At 53 and 46 days they weighed 400 and 307 g (14 and 10⁴/₅ oz) and were taking the same quantity of food as described for 48 and 41 days; the eldest had the body feathering almost complete.

At 68 and 61 days they weighed 415 and 333 g (14½ and 11¾ oz), respectively, and the eldest was becoming reluctant to take food. At 98 and 91 days they weighed 410 and 333 g (14⅔ and 11¾ oz): their weights had stabilized. Their weaning had commenced and they were offered pellets, bread and a

bird. During the breeding season the number of feedings is increased to five daily.

At Loro Parque the pair were originally housed in a stark aviary and seemed ill at ease. In August 1987 it became possible to move them into an aviary 17 m (50 ft) long, 2 m (6 ft) wide and 3 m (10 ft) high. The walls were built from concrete blocks; only part of the roof and the front of the aviary were constructed of welded mesh. Ivy grew up the walls, weeds several inches high flourished on the floor and a tree grew in the center of the aviary. The nest sites were located at the far end of the aviary: a palm log, a horizontal nest box and a vertical nest box. The birds have never damaged any of the growing vegetation; thus after a few months their enclosure felt and looked much more natural and the birds appeared more relaxed.

In January 1988 it appeared that they might nest. For a period of several weeks both birds spent most of their time in the palm log. Then they emerged and molted. However, I was confident that the female would lay the following year and in May a single egg was laid, which was broken.

Those who attended the meeting sponsored by the Parrot Working Group of the International Council for Bird Preservation (ICBP) and the International Union for the Conservation of Nature, held in Curitiba, Brazil in October 1988, heard much discussion about how the few Spix's in captivity in Brazil should be managed, and that a management agreement was being drawn up and a committee would be established. São Paulo Zoo had four specimens, two of which had been in the collection for 12 years – yet they had not even been sexed. In the same city, one of the best-known parrot breeders in Brazil, Nelson Kawall, had an egg-laying female. I saw this bird and an egg it had produced a few days prior to my visit in 1988. Those who attended the meeting heard Faiçal Simon, General Curator of the zoo, offer to lend

Nelson Kawall a male, if sexing revealed that one was in the zoo's collection. Nearly one year later, however, the birds still had not been sexed. (At least one offer had been made from overseas to do this at no charge to the zoo.)

There are few actual parrot *breeders* in Brazil. The only successes which had occurred with Spix's took place with Alvaro Rossman Carvalhaes in Santos, São Paulo, during the 1960s. At least eight young were reared in a tiny aviary, measuring 1.6 m (5 ft 6 in.) long, 1 m (3 ft 3 in.) wide and 2 m (6 ft 6 in.) high. Sadly, none of these birds survives today.

Outside of Brazil, the number of specimens documented in the avicultural literature of the past 50 years does not exceed single figures. In all probability, however, there are some "undocumented" specimens to which the owners are afraid to admit. In August 1987, Loro Parque in Tenerife inaugurated and sponsored a meeting with the approval of ICBP. The aim was to bring together the few holders of Spix's and to draw up recommendations for a long-term cooperative breeding program. The document was drawn up, but no owners could be persuaded to attend the meeting. Anxious to have owner-representatives from Brazil, the sponsors paid the cost of two air fares, but still no owners attended, even although a specific invitation was made to São Paulo Zoo. However, Carlos Keller, an exceptionally able Brazilian aviculturist, did attend and presented a paper on the Spix's situation. He pointed out:

Another fact that makes their reproduction in captivity difficult is that, as far as Spix's is concerned, there is very little exchange among breeders. This is easily explained when one considers the value of the bird. (I believe it is the highest priced bird in Brazil.) Generally, no breeder trusts another to the point of handing over his [bird] for reproduction purposes.

Another fact to bear in mind is that none of the Spix's Macaws outside Brazil have been legally exported from that country; thus the Brazilian Government is hardly likely to give permission for a bird already in captivity there to be sent abroad to make up a pair. This is understandable but does not help the situation in view of the fact that there is no one within Brazil who can match the expertise of the numerous specialist breeders of macaws in the United States and Europe.

All in all, the problems associated with establishing this critically endangered macaw in captivity appear almost insurmountable unless a way can be found to legalize all captive birds. Otherwise some will go "underground" and be lost forever from a potential cooperative breeding program. With such a small number of birds to work with, ultimate success will be impossible without the cooperation of every holder of a Spix's Macaw. These owners can consider themselves trustees of one of the world's treasures, trustees who *must* denounce all self-interest and consider only the future of this wonderful blue macaw.

Origin: northeastern Brazil. It occurs, or occurred in the recent past, in the following areas: southern Piaui, extreme southern Maranhao, northwestern Bahia, northeastern Goias and southwestern Pernambuco. In 1988 it was stated that the "last three" Spix's, which Paul Roth had been watching in Joazeiro, had been trapped. It was then believed that the species was extinct in the wild. Fortunately, this was not the case. At least three birds, including two young, were trapped in 1989.

Natural history: very little is known. Some indication of the bird's rarity can be gained from the fact that after the discovery of Spix's Macaw, by Spix in 1819 on the banks of the São Francisco River, over 80 years elapsed before this macaw was sighted again. On the next occasion Otmar Reiser observed some in 1903 near Parnagua. The extreme rarity of Spix's Macaw was not realized until the mid-1980s.

Probably the only people who have ever been familiar with the habits and behavior of Spix's Macaw are three or four trappers and literally one or two ornithologists. One of these, Paul Roth, told me that its preferred food is crabeira (*Tabebuia caraiba*). Roth studied the species in Curaça – descendants of the very same population from which Spix had taken the type specimen 166 years previously. It is believed that, during 1984, 12 Spix's were removed from this population. By 1988 all had gone. The tragedy is that most of them probably died fairly soon after being captured, probably because of an inadequate diet, and stress.

It is extremely disturbing that trappers alone know the locality of another population. These people cannot be expected to understand that, since the loss of the Curaça population, trapping of this species has become an international scandal.

Perhaps there is still hope. Carlos Keller, in the paper he presented at the meeting on Spix's Macaw in Tenerife, stated that he believed that the trappers have not yet penetrated deeply into the area in which this species is found. Brazil is vast and much of it remains unexplored. These facts lend credibility to the hope that this unique macaw will survive in areas as yet undiscovered by people.

12
Genus *Ara*

This is the genus to which 12 of the 17 macaw species belong (a thirteenth *Ara* species is extinct), and it can be said to contain all the "typical" macaws. The range in size and color of the species is varied and spectacular. All the *Ara* species are now well represented in aviculture, except Coulon's.

BLUE AND YELLOW MACAW
Ara ararauna
(Color pages 26/27)

Derivation: *Ara* comes from the Tupi Indian *ara*, meaning bird; the rest of the name is believed to be onomatopoeic, that is, it resembles the macaw's call.

Plumage: rich sky-blue above, golden-yellow below and beneath the wings. The forehead and forepart of the crown are dark green, the chin and throat black.

Length: 86 to 90 cm (34–36 in.) of which the tail accounts for at least half the total length.

Weight: males approximately 1,000 g (35 oz), but up to 1,200 g (42 oz) and females usually about 930 g (33 oz).

Soft parts: the partly bare facial area (decorated below and in front of the eye with lines of small black feathers) is white but can blush pink when the bird is excited. The feet are gray or black.

Beak and eyes: the beak is black and the iris is yellow.

Immature birds: differ in the color of the iris, which is gray (quickly becoming light yellowish gray). The tail is shorter in recently fledged birds but has attained its full length by the time they are five months old.

Abnormal coloration: specimens entirely devoid of yellow pigment, that is, blue and white, have been recorded. I saw one which had been obtained by an importer in London, on his premises, about 1973. Many years previously, one was exhibited at a small zoo in Entretat in France. In Germany, a pair, which produced a number of young lacking the blue pigment, was owned by Herr Bleil. The areas usually blue were brownish black. (A photograph of one of these birds appears in Low, 1986.)

Captive status: common – by far the most numerous of the large macaws. It is among the best known and most loved of tropical birds.

Pet potential: it is often kept as a pet. The temperament is variable: some are loving and affectionate, others are not to be trusted with anyone.

Breeding: this is the most prolific of the large macaws and perhaps second only to Illiger's among macaws in general. It is reared in good numbers in all countries where aviculture is practiced, except Australia. There, its extreme rarity makes it more expensive than a Hyacinthine would be in the United States. An indication of how easy it is to breed is given by the fact that in Caen, France, a pair hatched 25 young between 1818 and 1822, of which 15 were reared to maturity. In this era the breeding of parrots in captivity was almost unknown. This is the first captive breeding record for a member of the macaw family.

The tongue of a Blue and Yellow Macaw

The importance of compatibility of pairs has already been mentioned. It should therefore be emphasized, for those owners who read this with disbelief, that, under normal circumstances, all fit, compatible pairs are prolific. If they are not, something is wrong with their management, or they should be resexed. This species is an exception to the general rule that there are more males than females among macaws and other parrots. An extreme example of sex imbalance was related to me by Dr. G. Kaal, a Dutch veterinarian whose experience in the surgical sexing of parrots must be equaled by only two or three others in Europe. He once sexed 21 Blue and Yellow Macaws in a Dutch zoo. Twenty were females!

The clutch size is usually three or four, sometimes two. The usual interval between eggs is three days. Varying incubation periods have been recorded. Probably 25 days is the average, but numerous instances are given of 28-day incubation periods. However, not all these eggs usually hatched, and unless the eggs were marked when laid, the 28-day period may have been assumption rather than fact, the actual period being 25 days. On the other hand, in a cold climate 28 days is possible, just as a shorter period may occur in a hot climate. I have indisputable proof of an incubation period of only 24 days in the high temperatures of Gran Canaria. This is consistent.

Not only can the incubation period be short for a large parrot but the recycling period can be unbelievably brief. At Palmitos Park in Gran Canaria in 1989, a newly hatched chick and two eggs were removed from a pair on June 23 (because they failed to feed their chicks), 24 days after the first egg was laid. On July 5, only 12 days later, the female laid the first egg of the next clutch! The normal recycling period in macaws is three weeks.

Newly hatched chicks average 20 g in weight but there can be considerable variation above and below this weight. They have sparse white down on the head and back. The beak is pinkish, gradually darkening until, by the age of three weeks, it is mainly black; a little down remains, but the chicks have a very naked, pink appearance, and are also very shiny if parent-reared (or macaw-reared) as opposed to those that are hand-reared. The feathers of the throat, cheeks and forehead, and some of the wing coverts, are the first to erupt. Then comes the second down, which is grayish on the upperparts and white on the underparts. The birds are fully feathered, but with a short tail, by the age of about eight weeks. The young leave the nest between 90 and 100 days.

The correct size of band for this species is 14 mm. Chicks should be banded at 21–23 days if parent-reared, usually later if hand-reared. If banding is left too late for 14-mm bands to fit, 16-mm bands can safely be used (at about 30 days, if parent-reared). Weights of three macaw-reared chicks, when banded with 16-mm bands at 25, 28 and 31 days, were 696 g (24½ oz), 772 g (27¼ oz) and 858 g (30¼ oz). In each case this included about 60 g (2 oz) of food in the crop. The youngest chick was too large to be banded with a 14-mm band, yet the 16-mm band came off and had to be replaced one week later.

The Blue and Yellow Macaw is an extremely beautiful bird, very willing to breed and intelligent, and can make a loving pet. If it were rare, it would be one of the most expensive of all tropical birds. Do not underrate it because it is common and reasonably priced!

Origin: widely distributed over tropical South America, also Panama. From eastern Panama it ranges through northern Colombia, the entire Amazonian region, southern Venezuela and the Guianas; it occurs in northern Bolivia and central and northeastern Brazil, but is, of course, now extinct in coastal southeastern Brazil, where most of the forest has been destroyed. It occurs west of the Andes only in southwestern Ecuador. Old records of this species in Paraguay and Argentina possibly refer to birds which originated in Brazil and which were being traded.

Natural history: this is a lowland species, not usually found above 500 m (1,600 ft) or in hilly regions, except in Peru, where it may be found up to 1,500 m (5,000 ft). Its preferred habitats are varzea or gallery forest along rivers or lakes and around buriti palm (*Mauritia*) swamps. As well as feeding on the fruits of this and other species of palm, the birds often utilize hollows in dead palms as nesting sites. They may frequent palm swamps yet fly as much as 25 km (16 miles) to feed in secondary forest when a favorite food, such as the fruits of *Hura crepitans*, is ripe.

Of all the large macaws, this is the one most likely to be seen in the Amazon region and the Guianas and must be the most numerous over all.

Conservation: like all large macaws, the Blue and Yellow has declined or disappeared around centers of human habitation, especially large cities such as Belem in Brazil and Iquitos in Peru. Trapping and habitat degradation have caused its decline in the more accessible areas, especially on the edges of its range, such as eastern Panama. Since the 1970s, trade in this macaw has reached an unacceptably high level. For example, between October 1979 and June 1980, 2,635 were imported into the United States. Possibly 20,000 were taken from the wild to supply this number. In 1978, 1,173 were imported into the United States and the total for the first eight months of 1979 was 964. Although the United States is the main importer of this species, thousands more go to Europe and Japan. Some countries do have export quotas but these are much too high. For example, in 1986, the quota for Guyana was 3,370. It was recognized that this was too high and in 1988 the quota was reduced to 2,400 – still too high. In contrast, the export quota for Suriname in 1988 was only 200, a much more realistic figure.

More rigorous controls on the trade in wild-caught Blue and Yellow Macaws are essential for its survival. There are so many in captivity and the species breeds so well that there can be no justification for this trade.

BLUE-THROATED (CANINDE) MACAW
Ara glaucogularis **(formerly *Ara caninde*)**
(Color pages 30/31)

Derivation: *glauco* is from Greek, meaning light blue; *gularis* is from Latin, meaning throat.

Plumage: at a very quick glance this species could be mistaken for the Blue and Yellow Macaw, but it is immediately distinguished by its blue throat and by the more extensive throat markings: this area is black in the Blue and Yellow Macaw. The shade of yellow is also more orange than in the Blue and Yellow species. To my eyes, in a comparison of the two, all the details of *glaucogularis*, such as the finer, less massive head and beak, the more slender body and the

Blue-throated Macaws reared by the author at Loro Parque. The larger head and beak of the male (left) are typical of this species

intricacies of the plumage, have been designed to perfection by an artist, whereas *ararauna* looks as though it has been finished in a hurry! In *glaucogularis* the narrow lines of feathers on the cheeks are dark blue and extend over the entire cheeks, whereas in *ararauna* the cheeks are mainly bare. In *glaucogularis* the top of the head and upper surface of the body are entirely blue, whereas *ararauna* has the forehead green.

Weight: about 750 g (26 oz).

Length: 88 cm (35 in.).

Soft parts: the skin surrounding the lower mandible blushes a deep pink when the bird is excited, and is normally pale pink. This bare area forms a curved shape, similar to that of a Hyacinthine.

Beak and eyes: the beak is black and the iris of the eye is yellowish. The upper mandible is broader in the male.

Immature birds: differ from the adults in the color of the iris of the eye, which is grayish, gradually becoming yellowish by the age of one year. On fledging, young have a shorter tail, but within a couple of months the tail reaches adult length.

Captive status: rare and highly priced. Appendix I of CITES (since 1983).

Pet potential: this species should not even be considered: it is much too rare.

Breeding: unknown in aviculture until the late 1970s. The first captive breedings occurred in 1984, in the collection of Dr. B. Levine in Miami, Florida, and at Loro Parque, Tenerife, in the Canary Islands (Spain).

As curator of the Loro Parque collection for two years from February 1987, I had the good fortune to be responsible for the latter breeding pair. They were my favorite adult macaws in the park and ranked in my "top ten" of all the parrots there – over 1,500 from more than 200 species. The only macaws above them in this ranking were their 1987-hatched male and female offspring which I had the pleasure of hand-rearing in my apartment. Their wonderful temperament and beauty instilled in me a deep love for this species.

The breeding pair were obtained in 1981 and kept in a large aviary measuring 4 m (13 ft) × 3.6 m (12 ft) × about 3 m (10 ft) high. Two nest boxes were situated high in the aviary, one in each corner. During my time there, the female would lay her first clutch in the right-hand box and the second in the left-hand box. The birds reared a single youngster in 1984 and did not nest again until 1987. The first clutch was laid in May. Three chicks were hatched in two nests and removed for hand-rearing, but one died at an early age. Of the others, I reared one from the egg and the other from about eight days.

In 1988 the first clutch of three eggs was placed under a pair of Blue and Yellow Macaws. They were excellent foster parents but, for reasons undetermined, the eggs failed to hatch. As the *glaucogularis* had proved to be good parents, I was much happier about leaving the two eggs in the second clutch with them. One was infertile and the other hatched on June 20. The young bird left the nest during the second week of October. For the first few weeks it would sit high in a tree trunk in the middle of the aviary where there was no overhead cover. At night I would coax it to step onto a long pine branch and move it to the ladder which extended from the nest box to the floor. It would then return to the nest at night. (In high aviaries I always place such a ladder in position just before the young are due to fledge, to ensure they will not injure themselves on leaving the nest, and to enable them to return to it easily.)

At the time of writing, this macaw has been bred in at least six private collections in the United States and, in the United Kingdom, by Harry Sissen in Yorkshire. One private collection in the United States has the incredible nucleus of over 40 specimens. This collection is renowned for its breeding successes and therefore, in this instance, I believe this to be in the

Blue-throated Macaw bred by Harry Sissen

tropical savanna, with scattered "islands" of trees and ribbons of forest along the water courses. This savanna is inundated by rains from October until April. The breeding season is from November until March. Collectors took young birds from nesting cavities in trees in January or February – one or two per nest. One collector in the Monteverde region estimated the total population as 1,000 birds, while another, who collected over a much wider area, thought that the population numbered only about 500 – and that 50 of these were exported to the United States and ten to Europe in 1981.

Conservation: because this macaw was unknown in captivity until the late 1970s, when it was first trapped, the price was very high, which encouraged trappers to take as many as they could get. Trade was the sole threat to its existence and, in 1983, the species was placed on Appendix I of CITES. However, not all countries which import parrots are signatories to this treaty, and only a total ban on its export from Bolivia would (theoretically) protect it from trade. In May 1984 Bolivia instituted a ban on live animal exports, lifted the ban for a short while and then again prohibited export. Apparently, few Blue-throated Macaws have left Bolivia since then. There is no recent information on its status.

SCARLET MACAW
Ara macao
(Color pages 50/51)

Derivation: *macao* reputedly comes from the Portuguese *maçao*, meaning a large mallet. The sense is not clear.

Plumage: predominantly rich scarlet. It is recognized by the rich yellow of the central part of the wing, including the greater wing coverts, which gave rise to the old name of Red and Yellow Macaw. Primaries and secondaries are blue, and the lower back, rump and tail coverts are a very beautiful shade of light blue. The tail is scarlet, the shorter underfeathers being blue or

best interests of the species as it should ensure that it becomes well established in captivity. However, it was illegal trade, combined with the fact that the bird has a small population, that endangered this macaw.

The clutch size for this species is two or three. The incubation period is 26 days. Newly hatched chicks weigh about 18 g. Weights of the 1984 parent-reared chick at Loro Parque were as follows: 15 days, 387 g (13½ oz); 25 days, 510 g (18 oz); 38 days, 695 g (24½ oz); 50 days, 760 g (26⅘ oz); 71 days, 900 g (31⅘ oz). These weights were double those of the two I hand-reared and seem very high in view of the fact that at one year old the male weighed 771 g (27 oz) and the female 649 g (23 oz).

Origin: the Blue-throated Macaw has a small area of distribution: in the states of Beni and Santa Cruz in Bolivia. Earlier reports that it also occurred in Paraguay and Argentina are incorrect.

Natural history: this macaw prefers gallery forest along rivers and around lakes, generally in swampy, semiopen regions. The American ornithologist Dirk Lanning, who visited Bolivia in 1981, described its preferred habitat as humid lowlands in the

mainly blue. In captivity, the red will fade in birds which are exposed to strong sunlight.

Length: about 90 cm (35 in.).

Weight: approximately 900 to 1,000 g ($31^4/_5$–$38^4/_5$ oz).

Soft parts: the bare facial area is white and decorated, not with feathers, but with inconspicuous hairs. The bare skin has a regular pattern of small indentations.

Beak and eyes: the upper mandible is horn-colored, with a black cutting edge and a wider area of black near the base. The tip is gray. The lower mandible is black. The iris is pale yellow, usually with an inner ring of pale gray.

Immature birds: the tail is shorter than in adults, the iris is grayish and the lower mandible is gray at the time of fledging, having changed gradually from partly whitish and partly grayish.

Subspecies: no subspecies are recognized, but birds from the south of the range, from Brazil (and perhaps other localities), have the area of yellow on the wing substantially reduced; in some cases there is only one third as much yellow as in birds from more northerly areas. These southerly birds are also smaller. Rare in captivity outside Brazil, these birds probably occur only in that country. Illustrations in old books (e.g. Greene's; *Parrots in Captivity*, Vol. 11, 1884) mostly show the less colorful form.

Captive status: fairly common. The history of this species in trade and in captivity goes back hundreds of years. Outside the Americas it has always been one of the best known of tropical birds. Trade in wild-caught birds has, fortunately, been greatly reduced since this species was placed on Appendix I of CITES in 1985.

Pet potential: very young birds are suitable as pets until they are two years old. They should then be paired up in readiness for breeding. Adult birds are seldom gentle and affectionate; they tend to be aggressive and unreliable in temperament.

Breeding: when compatible pairs have been formed, they may prove extremely prolific. Pairs which are not truly compatible may not nest at all. A major problem for many breeders is locating a female, which are much scarcer in captivity than males.

Two to four eggs are laid. The incubation period is 24 or 25 days. Volk and Volk (1983) recorded an incubation period as short as 21 days in both incubator and with parents. Newly hatched chicks weigh 20 or 21 g and have some down, which is most prominent on the back.

Since the 1970s the Scarlet Macaw has been bred on countless occasions, in all the countries where aviculture is practiced, except Australia and New Zealand. The importation of exotic birds has been banned in these countries since 1959. Most of the Scarlet Macaws now offered for sale are captive-bred. A well-known breeder of this species in the United Kingdom is Robin Pickering. He has recorded that newly hatched chicks weigh 18 to 26.5 g (personal communication, 1986). He informed me:

Hens tend to lay in April or May and indicate imminent egg-laying with increased broodiness and copious large droppings. Clutch size is one to three eggs laid at two- to three-day intervals, although one had a six-day interval. Incubation commences with the first egg. I artificially incubate eggs at 37.7°C (100°F) with a low humidity. Average incubation takes 24.5 to 25 days. Chicks hatch with white to apricot down; down color varies in nest mates.

Development is as follows: the end of week 1, weight 38 g, lower mandible widened, almost shovel-like; week 2, 80 g [$2^4/_5$ oz]; week 3, 105 g [$3^4/_5$ oz], lower mandible darkening; week 4, 190 g [$6^4/_5$ oz), noticeable growth of head and wings, eyelids unfused; week 5, 370 g [13 oz], eyes and ears open, primary quills under skin; week 6, 520 g [$18^2/_5$ oz], quills broken through on wings and down quills on body; week 7, 675 g [23$^4/_5$ oz]; week 8, 790 g [27$^4/_5$ oz], becoming alert; week 9, 830 g [29¼ oz], feathering up; week 10, 850 g [30 oz], slimming phase, almost feathered, trying to fly; week 12, 875 g [30$^4/_5$ oz], sampling food, fully feathered; week 13, very active; week 14, 870 g [30¾ oz], flying. They are independent at 15 to 17 weeks; individuals vary. Hand-reared young are starting to talk.

Parent-reared young leave the nest at about 105 days.

Origin: occurring from eastern Mexico throughout much of tropical South America as far south as northern Bolivia, southern Peru and central Brazil, this is one of the most widely distributed of the macaws. It is found in Central America, Panama and northern Colombia. East of the Andes, it ranges through the Guianas, Brazil in the Orinoco and Amazon basins, central Brazil as far as northern Mato Grosso and northeastern Brazil in northwestern Maranhao. Since the nineteenth century its range has contracted, especially in Mexico, where it was extirpated from Tamaulipas. Since the 1930s it has disappeared from most of the Gulf slope lowlands in the states of Veracruz, Campeche and Tabasco (Ridgely, 1981) because of deforestation. Ridgely states of the Pacific coast: "It is only in the Selva Lacandona region of south-eastern Chiapas that a viable population of Scarlet Macaws still exists in Mexico. However, even this heretofore remote and untouched region has recently become accessible by a dirt road, and colonists have begun to move in."

Natural history: the Scarlet Macaw is declining rapidly in Central America. In Guatemala it remains numerous only in the Peten, and in El Salvador it is extinct. It may also be extinct on the Pacific coast of Honduras and Nicaragua. In Panama it is almost extinct on the mainland, being numerous only on Coiba Island (off

the Pacific coast). In November 1988, David Cameron Duffy, of the Centro de Documentación Biológica (National University) in Costa Rica, provided me with information on its status in that country. It exists in only three protected areas: Parque Nacional Corcovado, Parque Nacional Carara and El Refugio de Vida Silvestre Palo Verde. The last pair vanished from the Santa Rosa National Park several years ago.

David Cameron Duffy stated:

Population counts are speculative. Corcovado may have 500–2,000 pairs; Carara and the protected area to the south, 100 to 200 pairs and Palo Verde five pairs. I have yet to analyse data based on transects, but I am growing increasingly suspicious of the methods we use. If nothing else, they provide hard numbers which could be compared with future counts using the same methods.

There are also rumors of macaws in the central part of the north, but this is being cleared fast thanks to several new roads. Only the Corcovado population is likely to survive until the end of the century if present trends continue, although the conservation programmes may make for a brighter picture at Carara.

This macaw has been described as the most striking of tropical birds. This is so when it is seen perched, but is especially true in flight, with the magnificent long tail streaming behind it. Because of its wariness, it is more likely to be seen on the wing. The flight is steady and direct and sometimes takes it above the forest canopy. This is an enthralling sight for passengers in small aircraft.

This is a lowland species, not found above about 1,000 m (3,000 ft). It sometimes prefers open woodland, trees along river edges and savanna rather than dense forest. It feeds in the treetops on the fruits of licuri (*Syagus coronata*) and other palms, Brazil nuts (*Bertholletia exselsa*), jabillo

(*Hura crepitans*), *Lecythis* and jocote (*Spondias mombin*). Cultivated fruits, such as mangoes, are relished. According to Dr. J. Estudillo Lopez (1986): "Occasionally the Scarlet Macaw leaves the safety of the forest to visit coffee, maize, plantain and mango plantations which lie close to the forest; they do not generally cause much damage because it is only small groups which venture out."

The nest site is a hollow in a branch or trunk of a large tree, especially palms. A nest in a dead tree, discovered some years ago in Veracruz, Mexico, was situated about 10 m (30 ft) from the ground, at a point where the diameter of the tree was approximately 60 cm (2 ft). In the north of the range (Mexico) the breeding season commences at the end of March or the beginning of April; further south it starts about December.

Conservation: Three factors threaten the existence of the Scarlet Macaw: destruction of habitat (inevitably), international trade and local trade. Because of the enormous and fast-expanding human population in Mexico, the future of this species is bleak there. Only in areas away from human overpopulation, such as much of Amazonia, can it thrive.

International trade should no longer be a threat to its survival. Since it was placed on Appendix I of CITES, few wild-caught birds have reached Europe; however, no doubt they will continue to enter the United States illegally across the Mexican border. Because of the demand for its highly decorative tail feathers, a local trade in this macaw has existed for hundreds of years. They have been used in the ceremonial costumes of Indians of the southwestern states since at least AD 1100, it is believed. More than one scheme was launched in the 1980s to collect feathers from macaw owners and to sell or hire these out to Indians (see page 14).

GREEN-WINGED MACAW
Ara chloroptera
(Color pages 54/55)

Derivation: *chloro*, meaning green, (Greek *chlorós*); *ptera*, meaning wing (Greek *pterón*).

Plumage: head, underparts, under-wing coverts, part of the mantle and the tail deep red (of a darker shade than the Scarlet Macaw, from which it is immediately distinguished by the absence of yellow in the wings, giving rise to the old name of Red and Green Macaw). Greater wing coverts and secondaries are light blue and the outer webs of the primaries are dark blue. The back,

A Green-winged Macaw, aged 29 days, hatched at Loro Parque

A Green-winged Macaw chick aged about 11 weeks. The color of the lower mandible indicates its extreme immaturity

rump and tail coverts (upper and under) are a wonderful shade of light blue. The undersides of the tail and flight feathers are dark red. The secondary coverts and tertials are green.

Length: about 90 cm (36 in.).

Weight: a wide range between about 1,100 and 1,400 g (39 and 49 oz).

Soft parts: the bare white crinkled skin of the face is decorated with lines of small red feathers in front of, behind and beneath the eyes. The feet are gray.

Beak and eyes: the upper mandible is mainly pale horn color, with a wide black mark on the upper half of the cutting edge. The cere is feathered. The lower mandible is black. The color of the iris is pale yellow.

Immature birds: those which are fully feathered, but still in the nest, have the lower mandible whitish with a hint of pale gray; at fledging the lower mandible is partly dark gray, partly pale horn color. Before one year, the lower mandible is entirely black. At fledging, the iris is grayish, changing gradually to light yellow over a period of many months. The tail is shorter than in adult birds.

Captive status: common. Seldom fully appreciated, the Green-winged is, I believe, the most underrated of the family. Its beauty, more gentle temperament than the Scarlet (generally speaking) and intelligence make this a remarkable bird.

This species is believed to have been imported into Europe as early as the end of the sixteenth century. Despite its long history in captivity, however, captive breeding was rare until the 1980s. Previously, single birds were too often kept – and sadly abused and neglected in some cases. These are sensitive birds.

Pet potential: up to the age of two years, Green-wings, if obtained very young, make wonderful, affectionate pets. They then start to become much more independent and it is now time to sex them and pair them up. Two years is a good age to do this – no later, if possible.

Breeding: there are two main reasons for the dearth of breeding records: very few pairs were set up until the 1970s, and wild-caught birds seem to take longer to settle down or to mature than most large macaws.

The first breeding which definitely relates to the Green-wing took place in 1962 in the aviaries of the late J. S. Rigge of Millom, Cumbria, England. I will never forget seeing this pair in the mid-1960s. They were kept in an aviary constructed of 1.25-cm (½-in.) wire netting which they could have crushed with the same ease a person would tear paper, had they wished. They were obviously very contented birds. By 1984 this pair had reared 37 young.

In the United States the first breeding occurred in Texas in 1972, in the collection of another notable aviculturist, the late H. I. Gregory.

The clutch size of Green-wings is normally three, although very rarely do all three hatch. The usual interval between eggs is three days. Gregory recorded the incubation period as 27 days and a German breeder, G. Wilking, as 28 days. The higher temperature in Texas would explain the difference of one day.

The hatching weight of chicks is approximately 21 g. Young remain in the nest for about 14 weeks. One which hatched at Loro Parque, on June 5, 1988, left the nest on September 9 (96 days). If hand-reared, the young are gentle, affectionate and very sensitive and must be weaned very gradually. Total independence must not be expected before six months.

Origin: the range of this species, although still extensive, is declining. The Green-winged is already extinct in Argentina (probably since 1917) and in southeastern Brazil. It is now found in eastern Panama and throughout much of tropical South America, from northern Colombia across Venezuela, the Guianas and throughout most of Amazonia, to southeastern Peru, northern and eastern Bolivia, eastern Paraguay and eastern central Brazil, from the Mato Grosso east to Parana. It may still occur in other areas of Brazil.

Natural history: although this species is widespread, it is not numerous and is never seen in sizable flocks, except when congregating at clay licks. There have been serious declines on the margins of its range. In Panama, for example, it is now restricted to the most remote regions in the eastern third of the country

(Ridgely, 1981). The Darien National Park protects a critical habitat for this macaw. However, in southeastern Brazil it is extinct. The 22,000-hectare (85-sq-mi) Sooretama reserve was apparently not large enough to sustain it, and it disappeared here in 1964. This macaw still survives in substantial numbers in undisturbed areas of Amazonia and in the Guianas. Humid lowland forest, and foothills up to about 1,000 m (3,000 ft), are its favored habitat. It often occurs in the same area as the Scarlet Macaw.

Its diet includes large fruits and nuts, including those of such hard-shelled species as *Endopleura uchi*, *Hymenala* and the Brazil nut, *Bertholletia excelsa*. It is to be expected that the massive beak of the Green-wing (the fourth largest of any parrot) would be used to open hard-shelled fruits.

MILITARY MACAW
Ara militaris
(Color pages 58/59)

Derivation: the species name comes from the Latin *militaris*, meaning belonging to a soldier, the densely feathered red forehead, or perhaps the color combination, having some military significance.

Plumage: this species and Buffon's are the only large macaws which are mainly green (see under Buffon's Macaw for the features which distinguish the two).

Length: about 70–75 cm (27–29 in.), the birds from Mexico supposedly being slightly larger. They have been given the status of subspecies, *A. m. mexicana*, on this basis. The tail accounts for about one half of the total length.

Weight: approximately 900 g (31¾ oz).

Soft parts: the skin around the lower mandible blushes deep pink when the bird is excited. The feet are dark gray.

Beak and eyes: the beak is black and the iris of the eye is yellow with an inner ring of gray.

Immature birds: differ little from adults, except for the shorter tail on fledging, and the grayish eye.

Subspecies: *A. m. militaris*: the chin is brown. *A. m. mexicana*: slightly larger in size. *A. m. boliviana*: distinguished by the reddish brown throat.

Captive status: fairly common in the United States, less common elsewhere. The price is high outside the United States.

Pet potential: the often uncertain temperament of this species make it unsuitable as a pet.

Breeding: this macaw is, at present, being reared in comparatively few collections, although this situation is likely to change within the next few years. While the United States can be considered the stronghold of macaw-breeding this is not true of the Military. The proximity of the Mexican-Texan border has resulted in the smuggling of this macaw, which has tended to keep the price down, so that breeders have, unfortunately, concentrated on more profitable species. Elsewhere, the Military is much rarer and is among the higher-priced macaws.

There are no records of Military breeding until the early 1960s, and not until a decade later had more than half a dozen collections recorded success. In the TRAFFIC (USA) report, *Macaws: traded to extinction*, Nilsson and Mack (1980) compiled a table of macaws reared in American zoos between 1968 and 1977. Only nine Military were hatched. Six were reared.

The poor results for the Military reflect a lack of interest in the species at the time, not the fact that it is any more difficult to breed. While I was curator at Loro Parque, Tenerife, I had in my care a wonderful pair of Military Macaws which produced three clutches a year if two clutches were removed. They were exemplary parents.

In 1986 the pair had produced a single chick (their first, I believe) which was hand-reared. In 1987 the female laid three eggs in April. On May 2 two recently hatched chicks were removed from the nest, plus one egg. On hatching, the third chick weighed 21.7 g (22.3 g after the first feeding).

At first the food consisted of various cereals, including wheat germ, also sunflower seed kernels, peanut butter, alfalfa, carrot, apple, powdered calcium and liquid minerals, mixed in a blender with mineral water. This was later modified to increase the protein content. The elder two were removed from the hand-rearing room on August 16 when they were completely independent and desperately needed to be in an aviary so that they could exercise their wings. However, they did not react well to the change of location. Spoon-feeding was recommenced because they refused to feed. They started to eat a little when the food and water dishes were attached to the perch where they spent most of their time, but it was a month before they fed from the containers in the normal, lower position. For *seven* weeks I spoon-fed them early every morning. After a month they took only a little food but continued to crave the affection which went with it. I always had to spend some time in rubbing their heads!

One month after these two chicks and the egg were removed from the nest, the female laid again – this time two eggs. There was a newly hatched chick in the nest on July 9 and two chicks by July 11. These were left with the parents. The rearing period was totally uneventful. Because of the height of the nest box above the ground, about 3.7 m (12 ft), few nest inspections were made. Well before the young were expected to leave the nest, extra holders for pine tree branches were placed in the vicinity so that the nest box could be surrounded with pine branches. A ladder was placed from the nest to the ground. I hoped to avert any possible disaster when the young emerged from such a high nest.

The first young Military left the nest on September 28 at the amazingly early age of 81 days. It climbed down to one of the lower perches. Next day it did not appear. When it came out again, it remained near the nest for several days. I first saw the second young one out of the nest on October 13, aged 94 days. For the following week, when it did appear, it kept to the vicinity of the nest. Both young were very calm. In 1988 six young were reared from this pair, in three nests of two. Again, two were reared by the parents.

The only addition to the diet of the parents during the rearing period was bread and milk, usually with added calcium. They otherwise received the standard macaw diet at Loro Parque – a mixture of boiled maize, sprouted mung beans and chick peas, soaked sunflower seed, boiled peanuts, peanuts in the shell, peas and diced carrots (frozen, then thawed), also fresh apples, carrots and acelgar (similar to spinach), Brazil nuts, walnuts, oranges, bananas and, when available, the small fibrous orange fruits of a species of palm tree which was common in the park.

Origin: this macaw has a disjunct (not continuous) distribution. The subspecies known as *mexicana* occurs in central Mexico (southeastern) Sonora and southwestern Chihuahua southwards to the Isthmus of Tehuantepec and from southern Nuevo León and southern Tamaulipas as far south as the province of Mexico. The nominate subspecies, *militaris*, occurs in several areas of Colombia, as far north as Santa Marta in the Magdalena valley and extreme western Venezuela, and in Nariño, southern Colombia and the northern-central part of Ecuador. According to Fjeldsa, Krabbe and Ridgely's map (1987), its existence in southern Ecuador is uncertain; there may now be a break of several hundred miles in its distribution. This recommences in northern Peru. The doubtfully distinct *boliviana* inhabits Bolivia and northern Argentina (northern Salta). In Bolivia it is found in the extreme south, east of the Andes in Santa Cruz, Chuquisaca and Tarija.

Natural history: the Military Macaw is primarily a montane species. In Mexico, the Military inhabits semiarid temperate and tropical forests, close to streams, generally avoiding rain forest in the southeastern states, where it is replaced by the Scarlet Macaw (Estudillo Lopez, 1986). During spring and summer it is found as high as 2,500 m (8,200 ft) in the eastern and western Sierra Madre, where it visits forest of pine and ilex. In the winter it goes down to the depths of the great ravines and gullies of the Sierra Tarahumara, Cañon del Cobre and Cañada de Urique, for example, which are more than 2,000 m (6,000 ft) deep. During December to February, when there are heavy snowfalls on the peaks, it seeks out the tropical warmth of these ravines. It also visits the coast. Estudillo Lopez describes how these birds fly in flocks of 30 or more out of the breeding season

. . . which make a great din as they move from one place to another, returning at sunset to their resting areas. They usually visit salt-holes in the walls of some ravines in both ranges of mountains in search of minerals to balance their food ration, consisting of pine kernels, acorns, various fruits such as ficus, guavas, seeds and pods of the mesquite and leguminous matter, tender buds, etc. During the period when they visit the hot lands they eat palm fruits . . .

Estudillo Lopez states that the species's status varies according to the locality. Its numbers have diminished in Tamaulipas, where there is extensive agriculture and ranching. "Satisfactory" populations exist in the ravines of the western Sierra Madre, in Nayarit, Jalisco and Michoacan, but trapping for export has caused considerable damage to these populations. However, Mexico prohibited the export of birds shortly before Estudillo Lopez's report – and export has not recommenced.

The subspecies *militaris* is

generally found only above 1,000 m (3,000 ft). The sparsely inhabited mountainous Santa Marta region of northern Colombia is the only area where flocks of one hundred or more Military Macaws have been observed in recent years. In northern Peru the bird has declined because of deforestation. O'Neill (in Pasquier, 1981, "Comments on the Status of the Parrots Occurring in Peru") states that it is uncommon to common wherever cliffs are available for nesting, but very local. It occurred along the bases of the Andes.

Very little indeed is known about the subspecies *boliviana* but it is believed to have declined greatly in recent years. Its population may never have been large. Although the subspecies is quite rare in captivity, trapping has occurred and in the peak year (1982) of his macaw-collecting activities in Bolivia, Charles Cordier is said to have taken as many as 50 or 60. In Argentina, it was, in the past, recorded from Jujuy. Now it seems it occurs only in northern Salta, where it is rare.

The breeding season varies throughout the range. In Mexico it is from March to June; according to Hoppe (1985), that of the nominate subspecies starts in January to March and that of *boliviana* in November or December. Estudillo Lopez says that in Mexico the bird nests in large trunks of pines, as deep as 3 m (10 ft), also in hollows in rock faces "where various pairs congregate without apparent interference."

Conservation: this is dependent on three factors: protection of habitat, maintaining export bans (all of the countries in which this species occur have ceased to export birds), and curtailing the trade in feathers (see page 14). In Mexico it should survive in canyon areas because they have little agricultural value. In the south of Mexico and elsewhere in its range it will undoubtedly decline as human populations escalate.

BUFFON'S (GREAT GREEN) MACAW
Ara ambigua
(Color pages 62/63)

Buffon's Macaw reared at Paradise Park in Cornwall, England

Derivation: the species name is from the Latin *ambigua*, meaning doubtful or not clearly defined. Presumably Bechstein named it thus because he was uncertain whether it deserved specific status or whether it should be classified as a subspecies of *militaris*.

Plumage: the two are sometimes confused, especially if viewed at a distance. Close to, Buffon's should be easy to distinguish by its more massive head, beak and body, and by the lighter, more yellow shade of green. The tail color is also different, being mainly rusty-red to orange-red and blue at the tip (divided by yellow-orange in some specimens); in *militaris* the tail is mainly maroon and blue at the tip.

Length: about 85 cm (34 in.).

Weight: Harrison and Harrison (1986) give the average weight of 12 specimens as 1,290 g (45½ oz), the range being 1,186 to 1,594 g (42–56 oz).

Soft parts: the facial area is pink (deeper than in *militaris*), deepening to red when the bird blushes. The feet are dark gray.

Beak and eyes: the beak is black. The iris varies in adults from an indistinct pale yellowish color to dull yellow (very yellow in *militaris*).

Immature birds: differ from adults in having the iris brownish.

Subspecies: *Ara ambigua guayaquilensis* is said to differ in having the underside of the tail and flight feathers more greenish than in the nominate race, in which they are olive-yellow. The bill is said to be slightly smaller. However, Fjeldsa, Krabbe and Ridgely (1987) state that it is difficult to accept *guayaquilensis* as a valid race because of "the morphological overlap, both in bill size and colors, with nominate *ambigua*". They proposed synonymizing it.

Taxonomy: Buffon's Macaw (*Ara ambigua*) is generally accepted as a separate species, although its precise status has been the subject of speculation (e.g., Ridgely (1982) considered it and *militaris* closely related allospecies). Fjeldsa, Krabbe and Ridgely (1987) presented new information which made it appear that they could be conspecific (the same species), but added that the authors were not then "in a position to authoritatively state that the two taxa are in fact conspecific."

In 1983 Niels Krabbe and Paul Greenfield obtained a freshly shot *ambigua* from a local hunter at El Placer in the province of Esmeraldas, Ecuador, not far from the Colombian border but far from the Chongon Hills, the habitat of *guayaquilensis* (see under Origin, Buffon's Macaw). The area in between is now almost deforested but sightings in the provinces of Los Rios and Pichincha (cited in 1964 and 1978) are therefore more credible. These areas are between El Placier and the Chongon Hills.

The El Placer specimen was compared directly with 40 specimens of *ambigua* (including the type of *guayaquilensis*) and of the Military Macaw (including subspecies *mexicana*, *militaris* and *boliviana*). Four other specimens of *guayaquilensis* were available for comparison. Fjeldsa, Krabbe and Ridgely found that

. . . the color of the underside of wings and tail varied so much within each form that it could not be used for distinguishing Military from Great Green Macaw, Buffon's nor the subspecies of the latter. Furthermore, the red on the forehead and tail, the blue in the wings and tail, and the amount of maroon on the throat, foreneck and mid-belly, is subject to considerable variation in both subspecies of *A. ambigua*. This is of note, because these have been given as characters separating the subspecies *boliviana* from nominate *A. militaris* (Reichenow, 1908). The subspecific distinctness of *A. m. boliviana* had already been doubted by Zimmer (1930) and Bond and Meyer de Schauensee (1943). In addition, it appears that there are no real habitat differences between the two: it had been supposed that *A. militaris* was in general a bird of deciduous forest, *A. ambigua* of humid forest (Forshaw, 1973). *Militaris* occurs in humid forest in eastern Peru and eastern Ecuador, and *ambigua guayaquilensis* in deciduous forest in western Ecuador. In northern Peru the Military Macaw occurs both in deciduous (Koepcke, 1961) and humid forests (T. A. Parker, pers comm). Thus there seems to be

Buffon's Macaw has never been common in captivity and comparatively few breeding successes have occurred

Red-bellied Macaws

Eight-month-old
Red-bellied Macaw
reared at Loro
Parque, Tenerife

A six-day-old Red-bellied
Macaw chick

Red-bellied Macaw at 26
days when the beak is just
starting to darken

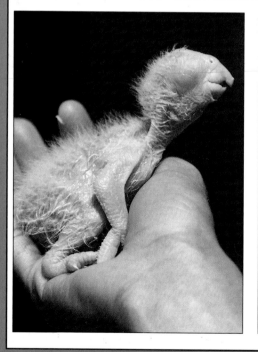

Red-bellied Macaws are the most difficult macaws to maintain and breed in captivity

no difference in habitat between Great Green Macaw and Military Macaw. . . .

Cytogenetics should provide some evidence regarding the relationship of these two forms. Jon Fjeldsa, coauthor of the paper referred to above, informed me: "To clear up the systematic question irrevocably, the right approach would be DNA sequence data on mitochondrial *and* nucleic DNA. Since the first is inherited matrilineally and the second is recombined for each generation, this combination will give the best evidence for stating hybridization. Using polymerase chain reaction (PCR), so little DNA is needed that it would be possible to obtain it from study skins."

Within the next few years it is probable that a number of laboratories of leading institutions and universities will commence this work; thus the relationships of many species will be clarified.

Captive status: rare. Existing in very small numbers, this species attracted little attention until the early 1980s. Until then, it had often been confused with the Military Macaw. In 1984 Buffon's was placed on Appendix I of CITES. It is now much sought after and very expensive.

Breeding: even now there are comparatively few pairs in aviculture. The first recorded breeding occurred in East Berlin Zoo in 1974. Remarkably, the pair was housed in an aviary 8 m (26 ft) square, with a pair of Military Macaws. The Buffon's nested in a hollow tree trunk and the Militarys on the aviary floor. The Buffon's hatched three chicks and reared two, and the Militarys hatched a single chick which was successfully reared (Grummt, 1986). In 1975, 1977 and 1979 single young Buffon's were raised. In 1984 four eggs were laid between May 29 and June 8. One egg was broken. Three hatched but two chicks died. The survivor was removed for hand-rearing at 34 days. From 1985 to 1989 one young one was reared each year.

The Avicultural Institute in California, under the direction of Dale Thompson, was very successful with this species. In 1984 and 1985, 11 were hatched. The average weight of newly hatched chicks was 22.6 g, the range being from 19.5 to 26 g. Average weights were as follows: day 1, 23.5 g ($^4/_5$ oz) (10 chicks); day 2, 26.4 g ($^9/_{10}$ oz) (10 chicks); day 3, 29.7 g (1 oz) (9); day 4, 34.3 g ($1^1/_5$ oz) (9); day 5, 39.0 g ($1^1/_3$ oz); day 6, 45.3 g ($1^3/_5$ oz); day 7, 52.5 g ($1^4/_5$ oz); day 14, 138.4 g ($4^9/_{10}$ oz); day 21, 313.5 g (11 oz); day 28, 630 g ($22^1/_4$ oz); day 35, 866 g ($50^1/_2$ oz); day 42, 1,074 g (38 oz) (8); day 49, 1,225 g ($43^1/_4$ oz) (7); day 56, 1,321 g ($46^3/_5$ oz) (5). Peak weight was 1,374 g ($48^1/_2$ oz) (4) at an average of 66 days. (Thompson, 1986.)

In the United Kingdom this macaw was first reared at Paradise Park (then Bird Paradise) in Cornwall in 1977. An egg, fostered to the nest of a pair of Scarlet Macaws, hatched and was reared for about ten weeks, when it was removed for hand-rearing. In later years, the Buffon's reared two chicks themselves.

It is regularly bred by Harry Sissen of Yorkshire and has been reared by John Stoodley of Hampshire.

In the United States it was not until 1982 that Buffon's was reared. This success was achieved by Dr. Nathan Gale and his wife. Two young were reared; both left the nest by the age of 12 weeks.

Origin: the nominate race is found from southeastern Honduras on the Caribbean slope of Central America, ranging through Nicaragua and Costa Rica to Panama, where it also occurs locally on the Pacific slope (Ridgely, 1981). In Colombia it is restricted to the Choco in the northwest. *A. a. guayaquilensis* was formerly known only from Guayas, southwestern Ecuador, but there is now evidence that it occurs, or once occurred, in other localities of western Ecuador (see notes on page 115 on taxonomy between Military and Buffon's Macaws).

Natural history: undisturbed humid lowland forest is the preferred habitat of this species. As this type of habitat is diminishing, this macaw, which is common only in very remote areas, can be expected to decline even further. It disappeared from the Canal Zone region of Panama in the early twentieth century. In 1977 it was confined to remote areas of the western and eastern thirds of Panama, the largest population being in Darien. However, because of construction of the Pan-American Highway, the capture of wild macaws there increased, especially in the Darien region, to which people had relocated from the Azuero Peninsula of central Panama. Delgado (1988) wrote:

> Macaws are now perceived by these immigrants as trade items, despite a prohibition on trade in protected species. Hunting for feathers is no longer confined to *Ara macao* and *A. ambigua*, having now extended to *A. ararauna* and *A. chloroptera*, species not found in Azuero. Macaws are also hunted for subsistence by indigenous people in the Darien region, perhaps adding to these pressures.

This macaw is observed in pairs or small groups only. Nesting starts in February or March in the north of its range. In the south, in Ecuador it starts to breed in January or earlier. Little is known about the Ecuadorian race. Ridgely (1981) states that it occurs in highly seasonal deciduous forest, at times venturing into mostly deforested areas to feed. The only region from which it is known with certainty is the Chongon Hills, west of Guayaquil. He described this as "virtually an island of forest in generally cleared country." The hills were, however, being invaded by colonists.

Conservation: this is mainly dependent on the protection of the forest. Given the present rate of destruction, its future looks bleak. Aviculturists can assist in two ways: by supporting the CIPA-ICBP program to collect tail feathers, and by ensuring that every bird in captivity has the opportunity to breed.

RED-FRONTED (RED-CHEEKED, LAFRESNAYE'S) MACAW
Ara rubrogenys
(Color page 82)

Derivation: *rubrogenys* is from the Latin and Greek: *rubro*, meaning red (Latin); *genys*, cheek (Greek).

Plumage: mainly olive-green. The forehead is red, merging into orange, and there is a red patch on the ear coverts. Red and orange are the colors of the shoulder; the carpal edge of the wing, under-wing coverts and thighs are orange, as are the feathers surrounding the vent. The primaries and primary coverts are grayish blue and the greater under-wing coverts are olive-yellow. The tail is green, bluish towards the tip, the underside being olive, and dusky at the tip. The lines of small feathers on the partly bare cheeks are blackish brown.

Length: about 60 cm (24 in.).

Weight: approximately 500 to 550 g (17½–19½ oz).

Soft parts: the skin surrounding the eye, and at the side of the lower mandible, is dark pink.

The Red-fronted Macaw was unknown in aviculture until 1973

Hahn's Macaw

Hahn's Macaw chicks aged four, six and ten days, hatched at Palmitos Park, Gran Canaria

Note the similarities in the coloration of the underwing coverts in an immature Hispaniolan Conure and (right) an immature Hahn's Macaw

Hahn's Macaws with two youngsters. This species is prolific – one pair reared six young in one nest

Breeding pair of Hahn's Macaws at Palmitos Park. The male, the lower bird, has a slightly larger head and beak

Beak and eyes: the beak is black and the iris of the eye yellow.

Immature birds: mainly green. The feathers of the forehead are brownish red and some of those on the abdomen pale orange. The red on the ear coverts is apparent as soon as chicks start to feather, whereas the red feathers on the forehead do not appear until the birds are aged six to 12 months.

Captive status: uncommon. It was unknown in aviculture until 1973, when very small numbers were exported to the United States and to Europe. The scandalous situation then developed where trade, and trade alone, was threatening the existence of this macaw. Most were destined for the United States where, by the early 1980s, trade had increased to the degree that supply outstripped demand and Red-fronted Macaws were being sold in pet shops. Official figures for the United States show the minimum numbers imported as follows: 1977, 16; 1978, 82; 1979, 125; 1980, 811; 1981, 210; 1982, 150. In view of the small range of this species, these numbers reflect trade of unacceptable proportions. Then, in 1983, the Red-fronted Macaw was placed on Appendix I of CITES and legal export to CITES signatory countries, such as the United States, ceased. However, birds continued to be smuggled out of Bolivia, destined for nonsignatory countries. In 1984 Bolivia instituted a ban on live animal exports, to operate for a year, and at the time of writing such a ban is again in operation. Fortunately, wild-caught Red-fronted Macaws are no longer offered for sale, but many captive-bred young are. This species has proved to be extremely prolific in some collections.

Pet potential: no doubt young hand-reared Red-fronted Macaws are being kept as pets in this country. Elsewhere they are considered as aviary birds and nothing has been recorded about their abilities as pets. Until they are extremely well established in aviculture, it would be wrong to promote this macaw as a pet bird.

Breeding: the Red-fronted Macaw is an ideal subject for captive breeding. Midway in size between the large and the dwarf macaws, it is within the scope of those people who are unable to house large and very noisy macaws. Being a mountain species, it is extremely hardy and, in the opinion of Harry Sissen, it tolerates cold, wet and windy conditions, for which tropical-zone parrots show a marked dislike. Its temperament is nervous but not aggressive, and in general it bites less than other macaws when handled. One of Harry Sissen's females broke off part of her upper mandible, necessitating syringe-feeding for several weeks. Although the bird was wild-caught and not tame,

A Red-fronted Macaw, aged about six and a half weeks, bred by Harry Sissen

after three or four feedings it demonstrated its intelligence or adaptability by readily allowing itself to be syringe-fed while still standing on the perch. It survived for six months on soft foods and broken walnuts before it was able to feed normally again.

Harry Sissen is the leading breeder of this species in the United Kingdom. His results demonstrate that it can be very prolific. Between 1984 and 1989 he and his wife reared 90 young. He now rears more than 20 every year, from four or five pairs. Some young are reared by the parents, and others by hand. His first success occurred in 1983, but the first U.K. breeding took place at Birdland, Bourton-on-the-Water in Gloucestershire, in 1981. The first recorded captive breeding took place at Wuppertal Zoo in West Germany in 1978, when three young were reared.

The Red-fronted Macaw usually lays three eggs. The incubation period is 26 days.

Origin: southern-central Bolivia, in the department of Cochabamba (southeastern part), western Santa Cruz, northern Chuquisaca and the eastern edge of Potosi (Lanning, 1982). The range is small.

Natural history: in 1970 a Red-fronted Macaw was taken to animal dealer Rolando Romero. After identifying it from skins in the British Museum (Natural History), he attempted to locate its habitat. At this time its precise range was unknown. In 1974 he located it in western Santa Cruz. The area is arid, remote and sparsely settled. There is shrubby vegetation, of the type associated with deserts, in the valleys and lower slopes, and taller woodland on some upper slopes and ridges. The macaws feed on the fruits of cactus, on the seeds of trees, on cultivated crops (including ripening corn on the cob) and on peanuts left in the fields after harvest.

Lanning (1982) estimated that the population consisted of between 3,000 and 5,000 birds. He believed that persecution and habitat destruction were

insignificant threats to the Red-fronted Macaw. Few residents possessed guns or nets; they did not eat the birds, use their feathers or keep them as pets. Little of this macaw's preferred habitat is suitable for agriculture, although the birds are unpopular with growers of corn and peanuts. Nevertheless, the local people are well aware of their value, and would be more likely to try to take them alive than to kill them. Their nesting sites are not vulnerable; they use sandstone cliffs which are inaccessible to collectors. Yet, in the space of a few years, the population was severely reduced – by trade. Lanning wrote: "Trapping of macaws for the export trade is the major threat to this species. Hundreds have been trapped and exported annually for the last several years (an estimated 300 in 1981), including both breeding adults and immatures."

One resident of Saipina, who showed him an active nest, told

Two Red-fronted Macaws at Palmitos Park

Hand-rearing

Welded mesh is the best surface for young macaws being hand-reared, such as this 34-day-old Blue and Yellow

When young macaws have been removed from the environment in which they have been reared, their food should at first be placed as close to the perch as possible

Fostering

Young Blue and Yellow Macaws with one foster parent (one of a pair of Green-winged Macaws)

Lanning that five to ten years previously he saw 200 or more macaws in the valley on a good day, but that the number had declined to 30 to 40.

Conservation: legal export from Bolivia has ceased because Bolivia has ceased to export birds (but this is no guarantee that trade will never recommence). As already mentioned, this macaw was placed on Appendix I of CITES in 1983. It might be naïve to suppose that trapping has ceased completely, but if illegal export still occurs, it must be on a very small scale compared with the previous trade. Therefore, as long as the Red-fronted's habitat remains intact and there is no persecution from local people, the population may regain its former strength.

CUBAN MACAW
Ara tricolor

EXTINCT

Derivation: the species name, *tricolor*, means three-colored (Latin).

Plumage: this very beautiful macaw had a red forehead, merging into yellowish red on the top of the head and shading into bright yellow on the nape. The feathers of the upper back were cinnamon-red, edged with greenish red. The entire underparts were scarlet, tinged with orange on the throat and also on the cheeks. The upper surface of the tail was cinnamon-red, shading into blue at the tip.

Length: about 46 cm (18 in.).

Weight: unknown.

Beak and eyes: the beak was black and the iris yellow.

Origin: Cuba, throughout the island except perhaps the province of Oriente. It was also found on the Isle of Pines, off Cuba.

Natural history: the last known specimen to be taken was shot at La Vega, near Cienaga de Zapata on the south coast, in 1864. However, in 1886 Cory wrote that the ornithologist Gundlach believed that a few Cuban Macaws survived in the swamps of southern Cuba. Its extinction was probably caused by capture for food and as pets, and due to the clearing of forest for agricultural purposes. These macaws apparently nested in palm trees and fed on fruits and seeds, especially those of palms and of the large flowering tree *Melia azdarach*.

Several hypothetical extinct macaws from the Caribbean have been described, but this is the only one whose existence is confirmed by the presence of skins in museums.

SEVERE (CHESTNUT-FRONTED) MACAW
Ara severa
(Color page 83)

Derivation: *severa* is from the Latin *severus*, referring to appearance.

Plumage: the chestnut forehead distinguishes the Severe from other macaws, as does its distinctive size. The forehead is tinged with blue, as is the crown; in some specimens crown and forehead *are* blue. Only one subspecies has been described, *castaneifrons*, which is said to be slightly larger overall. However, I am familiar with two Severe Macaws which differ significantly from those normally found in aviculture, and which presumably originate from Venezuela or Guyana. In these two birds the crown and forehead are blue, and some of the feathers of the upper breast and on the upper part of the wing are distinctly margined with bright blue.

The Severe Macaw has a brownish line of feathers bordering the lower part of the cheeks. The bend of the wing, carpal edge and under-wing coverts are scarlet. The tail feathers are reddish brown on the upper surface, edged with green towards the base and tipped with blue; on the underside they are pinkish red.

Length: about 49 cm (19 in.).

Weight: 360–410 g (12½–14½ oz).

Soft parts: the bare skin on the face is faintly yellowish white, decorated with about seven dotted lines of tiny black feathers. The feet are gray.

Except in the United States, the Severe Macaw is not common in captivity

Beak and eyes: the beak is black. The iris has a large inner ring of yellow and a brownish narrow outer ring.

Immature birds: the iris of the eye is grayish in very young birds, gradually becoming lighter.

Captive status: uncommon, except in the United States. From 1979 to 1982 a total of 4,870 Severe Macaws was imported into this country from Bolivia (TRAFFIC figures in Mores and Yzurieta, 1984), and 111 from other countries. Trade in this species continued for a few years more. However, outside the United States the Severe has never been common, and after Bolivia ceased to export it, trade virtually ceased, although Guyana, for example, was still exporting thousands of parrots.

Suriname, whose export quotas are generally considered a model for other exporting countries to follow, because of their realistically modest numbers, permitted the export of 238 Blue and Yellow Macaws and 66 Green-winged in its 1987 quota, yet only 38 Severes. This surely indicates that the species cannot be so common. Although its relatively dull plumage may make it less attractive to traders, the reduced availability of other macaws by the late 1980s meant that dealers were keen to obtain any macaw species.

Pet potential: young or hand-reared birds make good pets if given plenty of attention. It should be understood, however, that their voices are loud.

Breeding: the clutch usually consists of three eggs, sometimes two. Incubation periods of 24 to 26 days have been recorded and young spend ten to 12 weeks in the nest. Comparatively few breedings have occurred and little information is recorded in avicultural literature. In the United States this species was reared at San Diego Zoo as long ago as 1940, but the most consistent breeder has been Busch Gardens, Tampa, Florida, since 1977. In the United Kingdom it was first bred at Whipsnade Zoo in 1961 and has been consistently reared at Marwell Zoological Park in Hampshire since 1978. In Italy it was first bred at Naples Zoo in 1979.

In West Germany, in 1988, five members of the principal avicultural society, AZ, each with one pair, reared a total of 11 young. These included one pair belonging to Armin and Karin Brockner (1988). The birds were housed in an aviary which had indoor and outdoor sections, making a total length of 3 m (10 ft), 1.2 m (4 ft) wide and 2 m (6 ft) high. The base of the nest box measured 35 × 25 cm (14 × 10 in.)

Hybrids

Famous hybrid macaws, "King" and "Queen", at Parrot Jungle, Miami. "Queen" died in 1989 just before reaching the age of 49. They are seen here with the former owner of Parrot Jungle, Jerome Scherr

Hybridizing between Scarlet Macaws and Blue and Yellow Macaws regrettably occurs because of the shortage of Scarlet females and Blue and Yellow males

Trade in Feathers

Headdress used in the "Dirty Devils" dances in Panama, containing 65 macaw tail feathers. Trade in macaw feathers is yet another threat to the existence of wild macaws

A ten-week-old Severe Macaw bred by Armin and Karin Brockner of West Germany

and the entrance hole was 15 cm (6 in.) in diameter. The male and female were put together in March 1987. In the middle of July the female spent a long time in the nest. Two eggs were laid, one of which was fertile and hatched. At 12 weeks old the young Severe appeared at the nest entrance and seven days later it left the nest.

In 1989 Karin Brockner informed me that the clutch size of their pairs was normally three, and the incubation period about 26 days. Young usually spend 12 weeks in the nest. Their plumage is identical to that of adults. These birds proved loud and aggressive.

Another German aviculturist, H. Westen (1989), bred the Severe Macaw in 1988. The female laid two eggs, one of which hatched 25 days after the first was laid. The chick had sparse yellowish down. At 12 days its eyes started to open and it was banded at 18 days.

Origin: northern South America – the range covers an immense area. The nominate race (if one accepts that there are two subspecies) is found in Venezuela, Guyana, Suriname, French Guiana and Brazil (northwestern Mato Grosso, northern Goias and northwestern Bahia). *A. s. castaneifrons* occurs in eastern Panama, part of Venezuela, Colombia, eastern Peru, northern Bolivia and northwestern Brazil.

Natural history: Mainly a lowland species, it was recorded by Ridgely (1981) up to 1,500 m (5,000 ft) on the eastern slopes of the Andes in Napo, Ecuador,

although this may be a seasonal occurrence. Varzea forest, small clearings and forest edges are its preferred habitat, although in Venezuela it is also seen in gallery forest. Ridgely (1976) wrote that in Panama it apparently favors partially wooded areas, often those that are swampy, with many dead trees. At that time it was the macaw most likely to be seen in the Canal Zone area, and was fairly common in lowland forested regions in eastern Panama province. It formerly occurred westwards, to the Caribbean slope of the Canal Zone.

Among the foods eaten by this macaw are the fruits of fig and mango trees and cultivated maize crops. In the Manu National Park in Peru, Charles Munn (1988a) and his assistants observed Severe Macaws eating the following: the bark of *Ceiba pentandra*, the flowers of *Quararibea cordata*, the ripe fruit pulp of *Fevillea peruviana*, unripe or almost ripe seeds of *Sapium aereum* and mahogany, *Cedrela odorata*, the nectar from *Erythrina ulei*, whole

A Severe Macaw belonging to Armin and Karin Brockner

fruits of *Cecropia*, aril (seed covering) and seed of *Cupania cinerea* and fruit pulp and seeds of *Citharexylum poeppigii*.

Of two nests of this species found in Brazil, one was at a height of about 23 m (75 ft) above the ground and the other, in a Brazil nut tree (*Bertholletia excelsa*), was about 28 m (92 ft) high. One contained two chicks and a damaged egg.

Conservation: except in western Ecuador and in parts of Panama, where extensive deforestation has occurred, no special conservation measures seem necessary.

COULON'S (BLUE-HEADED) MACAW
Ara couloni

Derivation: the species is named after the Swiss natural historian Paul-Louis Coulon (1804–94), who was director of the natural history museum in Neuchatel.

Plumage: this is the only green macaw with the head entirely blue. The primaries and primary coverts are also blue; the secondaries and outermost upper-wing coverts are blue, margined with green. The tail feathers are reddish brown on the upperside, blue towards the tip and (as are the flight feathers) dusky yellow on the underside.

Soft parts: the bare facial area is gray-blue. The feet are flesh-colored.

Beak and eyes: the beak is gray-black; the iris yellow.

Immature birds: not described, but they probably differ from the adults only in having the iris grayish.

Captive status: always extremely rare and probably not represented in collections at the time of writing. Coulon's is the rarest of all the macaws in aviculture (if the Glaucous is not extinct). The only published records of it in captivity are those of Hoppe (1985), who states that this macaw was kept at West Berlin Zoo before the First World War, and of David West (1959), who kept a single male in California. Mills (1983) wrote that a few had been imported into the United States in the early 1980s; either they were short-lived or this was untrue as nothing has been published about these birds.

Pet potential: unknown.

Breeding: this has not occurred as it is doubtful whether there have ever been a male and a female in the same collection.

Origin: eastern Peru and possibly extreme southwestern Brazil. According to Ridgely (1981), it is found locally in the upper Huallage River valley, in Huanuco and southern San Martin, in the Ucayali River drainage, in southeastern Peru (southeastern Loreto–Balta on the Rio Curanja) and in Madre de Dios, near the border with northwestern Bolivia and possibly just across the border in Bolivia. It does occur in the Manu National Park in mature floodplain, hill and foothill forests, but is not common there.

Natural history: this macaw inhabits forest edges and clearings adjacent to woodland, even on the outskirts of towns such as Tingo Maria and Puerto Maldonado. The elevational range encompasses 150 to 1,300 m (500–4,260 ft).

In recent years, John P. O'Neill, from Louisiana State University, has observed Coulon's Macaw at Balta, 300 m (980 ft) above sea level. He saw pairs and threes.

Conservation: no measures are necessary as no threats to its survival are known. Ridgeley even wrote: "It is quite possible that in coming decades *Ara couloni* may even increase and spread, as settlers move into many heretofore uninhabited areas." He apparently believed that small-scale agriculture would be beneficial to this macaw.

ILLIGER'S MACAW
Ara maracana
(Color pages 86, 87, 90, 91)

Derivation: *maracana* is a South American Indian word for a large parakeet or small macaw.

Plumage: This is the only small macaw in which adults have the forehead red (a small area, not extending to the crown). The remainder of the head is dark blue, becoming more greenish blue towards the nape. On the abdomen there is a variable U-shaped red patch; the lower back is also red. The primaries and their coverts, and the secondaries, are blue. The tail feathers are maroon on the basal half (with some olive-green) and mainly blue (and some golden-olive) elsewhere; underside is olive-yellow and blackish.

Length: 41 cm (15½ in.).

Weight: average 250 to 280 g ($8^4/_5$–$9^4/_5$ oz).

Soft parts: the bare skin of the face is whitish, faintly tinged yellow and decorated with lines of fine black hairs. The feet are flesh-colored.

Beak and eyes: the beak is black and the iris reddish brown.

Immature birds: usually have less red on the forehead, with softer colors on the head and, on fledging, slightly shorter tails. The iris is dark brown, soon changing to reddish brown, and the feet are grayish, then dark gray, taking longer to change to adult color than the iris.

Mutations: a Dilute Yellow was bred in 1978 from a pair of Illiger's belonging to G. A. Smith of Peterborough, England. It was mainly cream-colored. The parents were brother and sister (inbreeding increases the chance of producing a mutation). In 1988 a Cinnamon

Illiger's was hatched at Busch Gardens, Tampa, Florida. It was pale yellow-green, with a brownish forehead and red on the abdomen. The beak was brownish black.

Captive status: fairly common. When other macaws were being traded in large numbers, export figures for Illiger's were low. Numbers imported into the United States were as follows: 1970, 136; 1971, 461; 1972, 51; 1974, 91; 1977, 113; 1978, 41 (figures are incomplete for the years 1970, 1971, 1975 and 1976) (Nilsson and Mack, 1980). Illiger's was the only *Ara* macaw, apart from the elusive Coulon's, not imported into the United States between 1979 and 1982. Paraguay was the main exporting country of this species. Export has now ceased but, because this small macaw is free-breeding, it is well represented in aviculture.

Pet potential: good, because of this bird's small size, intelligence and ability to mimic. Hand-reared birds can be fearless and noisy.

Breeding: Illiger's is certainly the most prolific of the small macaws and probably ties for first place with the Blue and Yellow among the macaws in general. A pair belonging to Mrs. O. Oakes in Suffolk, England, reared 120 young between 1978 and 1989.

This species usually lays three eggs, sometimes four. The interval

Illiger's Macaw aged 46 days, but not yet fully feathered

Illiger's Macaw, the only small species on Appendix 1 of CITES (since 1989)

advisable to hold them with one hand around the wings.

Origin: eastern Brazil, eastern Paraguay and northeastern Argentina (Misiones). In Brazil Illiger's is said to occur from southern Para and Maranhao south to the coastal region from southern Bahia to Rio Grande do Sul. Ridgely (1981) stated that in 1980, in southeastern Brazil, it survived only in a few remnant forests.

Natural history: little is known or recorded about this species, which is believed to have undergone a very serious population decline in recent years. Ridgely (1981) recommended protection of forest tracts in Paraguay where Illiger's then occurred, but nothing was done, and no population studies were carried out in any part of its range. By 1989 it was being considered for Appendix I of CITES. In the paper from Paraguay proposing this, it was stated that Illiger's was one of the least known parrots of the neotropics, that almost nothing was known about its feeding or breeding habits and that it was difficult to investigate because of its rarity. The proposers quoted Nores and Yzurieta (1983), who could find only eight or ten specimens in the Argentinian departments of Canendiyu and Amambay, and Lopez, who, in 1989, could find only one pair in the department of Concepcion after being in the field for eight months. There were no sightings at all for Argentina.

Little is known about Illiger's status in Brazil, where its decline must have been rapid because of habitat destruction. Hoppe (1985) quoted Gomez, who, in the early 1960s, saw large flocks in the vicinity of São Paulo, but by the early 1980s had not seen groups larger than 20 birds.

Conservation: the first step should be to investigate this macaw's status in different parts of its range and the reasons for its decline. If it is already as rare as some fear, its prolificacy in captivity may be its salvation.

between eggs is normally three days. From marking the eggs as laid by two pairs at Palmitos Park, Gran Canaria, and from my notes of one pair at Loro Parque, Tenerife, I know that the incubation period of the first egg in the clutch is 24 to 26 days; in one pair at Palmitos Park and the only egg, apart from the first in the clutch, for which I have data on the Loro Parque pair, the incubation period for subsequent eggs was 23 days. In the second pair at Palmitos Park, the incubation period for subsequent eggs was 24 days. Newly hatched chicks weigh 11 g.

The age at which young have left the nest has been recorded as from three months to 14 weeks in the cool climate of western Europe. At Loro Parque two young left one nest at only 66 and 68 days, and another nest at 68 and 71 days. At Palmitos Park, young fledged between 57 and 65 days.

Young put on weight quickly and the adult weight is reached at about 28 days.

The character of this species is not improved by hand-rearing. The resulting young are not affectionate or endearing. During spoon-feeding, the strong wing movement of some chicks makes it

YELLOW-COLLARED (YELLOW-NAPED) MACAW
Ara auricollis
(Color pages 94, 95)

Derivation: The species name is derived from the Latin: *auri*, meaning gold; *collis*, neck.

Plumage: mainly dark green with a yellow collar encircling two-thirds of the neck in contrast to the green-and-black head and nape. The primaries are blue and the undersides of wings and tail are golden-olive. The upper surface of the tail is maroon near the base and blue and green towards the tip.

Length: about 40 cm (16 in.).

Weight: about 250 g ($8^4/_5$ oz).

Soft parts: bare skin on the cheeks and surrounding the eyes is white with rows of tiny, hairlike feathers on part of the cheeks, which are not very noticeable. The feet are pinkish.

Beak and eyes: the beak is black, whitish at the tip of the lower mandible. The iris of the eye is reddish brown.

Immature birds: differ only in their grayish feet and grayish iris, the outer ring of which becomes brown at an early age, approximately three and a half months (must be viewed in good light). The culmen (dorsal ridge of the upper mandible) is whitish.

Captive status: very rare in aviculture until the early 1970s; now it is not uncommon. For example, commercial importation into the United Kingdom commenced in 1973 with 20 birds; in 1976, 217 were imported. The minimum numbers imported into the United States after 1973 were as follows for random years: 1974, 120; 1978, 1,666; 1981, 2,518 (data from TRAFFIC). The Yellow-collared is popular and frequently bred in the United States, less so elsewhere.

Pet potential: excellent. Hand-reared birds are affectionate or forceful, are playful, and readily learn to mimic; other young birds are easily tamed. Their size makes them suitable for apartments and their voices are pleasant by macaw standards.

Breeding: The Yellow-collared Macaw nests readily in captivity. The nest box need not be large. The pair at Palmitos Park use a box measuring approximately 25 cm (10 in.) square and 61 cm (2 ft) high while those belonging to Mrs. Olivia Oakes in England used a box measuring 36 cm (14 in.) square and 51 cm (20 in.) high. The entrance should be about 7 cm (2¾ in.) in diameter. The clutch size is usually three, sometimes four. The incubation period is 24 to 26 days.

Weights of chicks hatched by a pair belonging to G. A. Smith were 11.8, 12 and 13 g. Newly hatched chicks have shortish white down on head and body, which is fairly dense for a macaw. Chicks soon lose the first down and are virtually naked until the feathers start to erupt at about three weeks. Young leave the nest between ten and 11 weeks.

The pair at Palmitos Park, Gran Canaria, have been breeding since 1988. In 1989 the first two chicks hatched on February 15 and 17.

The Yellow-collared Macaw makes an excellent pet and readily learns to talk if obtained when young

The third chick, which was smaller and weaker than the others, was removed for hand-rearing on March 3 and was weaned by the first week of June. The parent-reared young were removed from their parents on June 6, having left the nest on April 24.

Eggs of the next clutch were laid on June 21, 24, 27 and 30. In each case the incubation period was 24 days, the chicks hatching on July 15, 18, 21 and 24. The fourth egg was transferred to the nest of a pair of Sun Conures (*Aratinga solstitialsis*) which had their very first clutch of eggs. The Yellow-collared chick hatched five days before the first conure chick.

All four *auricollis* eggs started to pip about 48 hours before they hatched. On the day the third egg hatched (when the eldest was six days old and the second three days old), the first weighed 41 g (1⅔ oz) with a full crop, the second 28 g with a little food in its crop and the newly hatched chick 13 g with a little liquid food in its crop. One week later (July 28) they weighed 104, 88 and 48 g ($3^7/_{10}$, 3 and $1^7/_{10}$ oz). All had full crops. The eyes of the eldest were half-open and the ears were still closed.

On August 8, when they were aged 26, 23 and 20 days, the eldest weighed 216 g (7½ oz); its wing coverts and tail feathers measured 180 mm (¾ in.) and its feet were gray. The second chick was the same weight, the erupted feathers were half the length of those of the older chick and the feet were spotted with pink and gray. The third chick weighed 176 g (6 oz) with the crop full, its ears were open and the tail feathers (the first to erupt) were just showing. Six days later the chicks weighed: 238 g (8½ oz), with crop two-thirds full (32 days); 236 g (8 oz) with full crop (29 days); 214 g (7½ oz) with crop two-thirds full (26 days). One week later they had attained or were approaching their maximum weights. The eldest (39 days) weighed 242 g (8½ oz), the second 248 g (8⁴/₅ oz) and the third 238 g (8½ oz); all had some food in the crop, perhaps 12 g.

Origin: northern and eastern Bolivia, ranging eastwards into Brazil to the Mato Grosso and southwards into northern Paraguay and Jujuy and Salta in northwestern Argentina.

Natural history: this macaw occurs in varying types of habitat, according to Ridgely (1981), ranging from humid upper tropical forest at the base of the Andes in Salta, through deciduous chaco woodland over much of its range, to cerrado and pantanal with gallery forest in Mato Grosso and Goias. Primarily a bird of the lowlands, it does occur up to about 600 m (2,000 ft) in northwestern Argentina.

Little is known about the natural history of this species, which is believed to be common throughout most of its range. Much of this has not been modified by people; however, it can also exist in areas where extensive habitat modification has occurred, such as agricultural regions in the vicinity of large cities (e.g., Santa Cruz in Bolivia). Nores and Yzurieta (1984) foresaw a rapid decline in its population in Bolivia if capture for export continued. This ceased in May 1984 but commenced again for a short while; then export of all Bolivian birds was prohibited once more and is not likely to recommence.

The Yellow-collared Macaw was *formerly* found in enormous flocks in Bolivia. It was one of the commonest birds when Goodfellow (1933) lived there. He described a clearing with

> . . . a number of small water holes and some swampy ground never dry. It was to these that the Macaws came in their hundreds morning and evening, when every tree around the damp parts was literally covered with them, wherever a foothold was to be had.

Goodfellow presented two Yellow-collared Macaws to London Zoo in 1920. He believed that they were the first live specimens to reach Europe.

Conservation: now that trade in

wild-caught birds has ceased, destruction of habitat will be the main threat to this species. There are insufficient protected areas within its range; thus it is fortunate that the Yellow-collared is able to survive in disturbed habitats.

RED-BELLIED MACAW
Ara manilata
(Color pages 114/115)

Derivation: unknown.

Plumage: mainly green with the abdomen maroon. The crown is greenish blue. The feathers of the breast and part of the abdomen are margined with blue-gray, giving a soft bluish tinge to the underparts. The under-wing coverts are olive or yellowish green and the undersides of the tail and flight feathers are olive-yellow. An inconspicuous line of small black feathers borders the naked facial skin above the cheeks.

Length: 46 cm (18 in.).

Weight: 280–300 g (10–10½ oz).

Soft parts: it is the large area of parchment-yellow naked skin on the face which gives this macaw such a distinctive appearance. The feet are gray.

Beak and eyes: the beak is black and the iris is dark brown.

Immature birds: differ from the adults in having the facial skin whitish yellow, i.e., paler. The upper mandible is not entirely black, the culmen is whitish; the lower mandible is light and dark gray. The head is merely tinged with blue. The feet are gray.

Captive status: uncommon. Although regularly offered for sale in Europe from 1985, trade has been on a small scale. The largest numbers imported into the United States up to 1982, for example, were 383 in 1981 and 219 in 1982. Previously, the numbers had probably not exceeded 100 in any one year and none were recorded between 1968 and 1972 (Nilsson and Mack, 1980). Much smaller numbers were imported into the United Kingdom, perhaps fewer than 200 during the 1970s.

Pet potential: poor, for two reasons. First, this species has a very nervous temperament.

Wild-caught birds are easily stressed and my experience of the captive-bred parent-reared young from one very prolific pair suggests that they are aloof. Second, if caged, this species appears to be more prone to obesity than any other macaw. Five young parent-reared birds at Loro Parque were placed in a 3-m (10-ft) long suspended cage after being removed from their parents. By about six months old, however, they were so fat that they had to be released into a 17-m (50-ft) long flight to obtain flying exercise. At first, they were unable to fly. They were fed on the same diet as other neotropical parrots in the collection. Andrew Greenwood, a leading avian veterinarian in the United Kingdom, examined two Red-bellied Macaws at postmortems on different occasions. Both were apparently in good health but had died suddenly. He discovered that they were extremely fat and had died from acute heart failure, with severe atherosclerosis and fatty and degenerative changes in the heart muscle.

The Red-bellied Macaw is the only macaw in which wild-caught birds do not readily adapt to captivity

Breeding: this is the most rarely bred of the available *Ara* macaws. The first recorded breeding occurred in the collection of Florida veterinarian Greg Harrison in July 1982. The second breeder, and the first in the United Kingdom, was Mrs. Phyllis Vahrman of Cornwall. While living in Guyana she observed how active these birds were. She informed me:

My pair are completely tame and very confident in their environment, which is an unusual one. I keep my birds free in a very large parrot house measuring about 13.2 m (44 ft) × 3.6 m (12 ft). It is furnished with hanging branches and plants. The cock seems to have to range widely and to forage when the hen is incubating – she sits very tightly and I rarely see her.

In 1985 the pair produced four clutches of infertile eggs. In 1986 they chose a different nest box, measuring about 31 cm (12 in.) square. Three eggs were laid, one of which hatched on March 13. In addition to the usual foods, a rearing food was offered which consisted of yolk of egg, frozen peas, grated raw carrot, stoneground wholemeal bread, unsweetened crackers, the kernels of pine nuts and honey water, and also SMA, a mineral and vitamin supplement in powder form. The food was situated on different levels and in different places so that the birds had to search for it. In 1986 one chick was reared.

I had the good fortune to be responsible for two years for the pair which must surely be the most prolific in captivity to date – at Loro Parque, Tenerife. The species was represented by two males on exhibit and by a pair off exhibit in an aviary measuring approximately 4 m (13 ft) long, 1 m (3 ft 4 in.) wide and 2.1 m (7 ft) high. Their nest box measured 31 cm (12 in.) × 33 cm (13 in.) × 76 cm (30 in.) high.

The female laid four eggs in April 1987. There were two eggs on April 7. On April 22 one egg was placed in an incubator. It hatched in the incubator at 5 p.m. on April 30 and, two hours later, the chick was transferred to the nest of a pair of Illiger's Macaws which were known to be excellent parents. They had two chicks, about two and three days old, and immediately accepted the *manilata* chick. The next day there was a pip mark on another egg, which was removed to the incubator. The chick hatched on May 3 and it, too, was transferred to the nest of the Illiger's. Their eldest chick was taken for hand-rearing, as was an egg which hatched later that day. The third *manilata* egg pipped and hatched in the incubator on May 7. It weighed 13.2 g.

The two chicks with the Illiger's thrived and were banded at 19 and 21 days with 10-mm bands (9-mm would have been better). The first

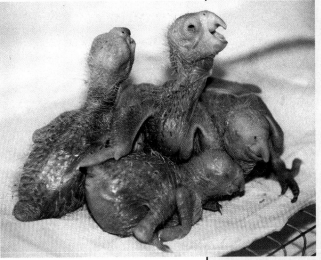

chick left the nest on July 17, aged 79 days, and the second on July 19, aged 77 days.

The appearance of the chicks was as follows: day 1, fairly long yellowish down on the upperparts and head; down shorter and more whitish on the underparts. The beak was whitish and the nails white. Day 19, eyes open; ears just open. The beak was pinkish white. The head was bare, the skin having an almost wrinkled appearance. No feathers had erupted but there were prominent dark lines under the skin of the developing feathers or, on the back, developing second down. A little short whitish down

Four Red-bellied chicks aged 10 to 18 days – from probably the most prolific pair in captivity, at Loro Parque

remained on the back and nape. Tail quills were present, and wing feathers in quills, 1.2 to 2.5 cm (½–1 in.) long. Day 26, the soft pads on the side of the beak were dark; the beak was otherwise white, tinged with gray. The head was almost bare. Sparse tufts of gray second down were on the back; the wing feathers were erupting. Day 40, the wings were nearly fully feathered; the back and sides of neck were bare; the crop and underparts were virtually bare. Day 46, the head and wings were three-quarters feathered. Day 49, the head feathers were bluish; the bird was almost completely feathered. The bare skin on the face was white. The beak was white, with gray at the base of the upper mandible and on the raised pads. The feet and nails were gray.

The two young Red-bellied Macaws and their Illiger's companion were removed to a suspended cage on August 10. At that stage, fresh corn on the cob was their favorite food. Bread and milk had been taken by the parents during the rearing period, plus plenty of fresh corn on the cob and the usual food, which consisted of soaked or sprouted sunflower seed, boiled maize, sprouted mung beans, boiled peanut kernels, apples, carrots and Swiss chard. Other fruits in season, such as pears, palm fruits and cactus fruits, were offered.

The eggs from the first clutch had been removed at the beginning of May. Three eggs were laid in the second clutch, one of which (probably the last) was infertile. The first egg was laid on June 1 and there were two chicks by June 27, giving an incubation period of 25 days. The young first left the nest on September 8 but, for the next few days, spent much of the time inside the nest.

In 1988 the first of four eggs was laid on February 14. All four hatched, probably on March 10, 12 and 14, and the fourth after the sixteenth. The birds were removed for hand-rearing on March 21.

In the second clutch, the first of three eggs was laid by May 1.

There was one chick on May 26, two on May 28 and three on May 30. They left the nest at the end of August.

In 1989 two chicks hatched in the first nest.

Origin: northeastern Colombia, eastern Venezuela and the Guianas south to central and northeastern Brazil, as far as Mato Grosso, Goias, western Bahia and Piaui and, to the west, as far as northern Bolivia. This macaw also inhabits Trinidad.

Natural history: this is a lowland species which occurs only in humid areas in association with the buriti palm (*Mauritia flexuosa*), the pulp of the fruits and blossoms of which forms the major item of its diet. This palm is found no further south than Minas Gerais in Brazil. According to Paul Roth, the Red-bellied Macaw is almost totally dependent on it. Roth, a Swiss ornithologist, is one of the most highly experienced field workers with neotropical parrots. Speaking at the ICBP/Parrot Working Group meeting in Curitiba, Brazil, in October 1988, he said that for five or six months of the year the availability of these fruits is high and the young Red-bellied Macaws fledge just before this season.

According to Ridgely (1981), this macaw rarely even perches in other trees. "Stands of these palms are found locally in swampy or seasonally flooded terrain in regions that otherwise vary from being forested to semi-open (savanna or cerrado)." The Red-bellied Macaw is therefore local in distribution but common in some areas. In certain regions, such as northwestern Meta in Colombia, and in the Zona Bragantina, east of Belem in Brazil, the Red-bellied was, in 1980 (and still may be), found in regions from where all other macaws have long since been extirpated.

Conservation: as long as groves of buriti palms survive, so will the Red-bellied Macaw. There does not appear to be any particular commercial demand for this palm at the present time.

13
Genus *Diopsittaca*

This genus has been reinstated recently by taxonomists who believe that the small species more often known as *Ara nobilis* does not belong in the genus *Ara*. I agree with this view. *Diopsittaca* was originally named by Ridgway in 1912. He separated *nobilis* on account of the reduced area of bare skin on the face and the small overall size of the bird. While his reasons may be arguable, there are other points to be considered, factors which indicate that *nobilis* has similarities with the genus *Aratinga*. Indeed, it can be considered as the species which links the two genera.

It is more akin to the genus *Aratinga* in the following respects:

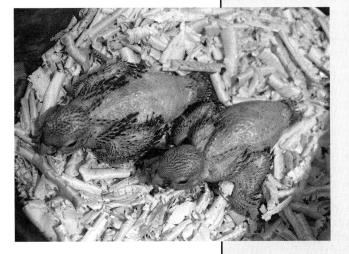

1 The immature plumage differs significantly from that of the adult, as it does in most *Aratinga* species, especially the larger species with red in their plumage, but not the group or superspecies of *solstitialis*, *jandaya* and *auricapilla*. In the adult *nobilis*, the bend of the wing and the under-wing coverts are red. This is also true of the Hispaniolan Conure (*A. chloroptera*), which reminds me very much of *nobilis*. In immatures of both species, the bend of the wing is green and the under-wing coverts are mainly green or margined with red.

2 Young *nobilis* spend only eight weeks in the nest, like *Aratinga*, but unlike *Ara*, chicks, which remain for at least ten weeks.

3 Hoppe (1985) points out that

If these Hispaniolan Conure chicks had not been denuded of down by their parents, they would bear a remarkable similarity to the young of Hahn's Macaw

Hahn's Macaw aged 41 days and bearing a strong resemblance to some of the larger *Aratinga* Conures

during the nonbreeding season *nobilis* flies in large flocks, whereas other macaws forage only in pairs, family groups or small flocks, except when they congregate at salt licks or clay deposits, when several species may be present. He suggests that this behavior shows the close relationship to *Aratinga* species, which move about in large flocks.

HAHN'S MACAW
Diopsittaca nobilis nobilis
(Color pages 118/119)

NOBLE MACAW
Diopsittaca nobilis cumanensis

Derivation: *Diopsittaca* is from the Greek: *dio* (stately, splendid); *psittaca* (parrot); *nobilis*, means noble (Latin); *cumanensis* means of the bay of Cuman (Maranhao, eastern Brazil).

Hahn's Macaw
Plumage: uniform green (mid- to dark green), except the forehead and forepart of the crown, which are blue. The bend of the wing, the carpal edge and the under-wing coverts are red.
   Length: 31 cm (12 in.).
   Weight: about 165 g (5^4/$_5$ oz).
   Soft parts: the bare skin on the face is white, with tiny black dots of feathers. The feet are dark gray.
   Beak and eyes: the upper and lower mandibles are black. The iris is reddish brown.
   Immature birds: have the feathers of the forehead broadly margined with dark gray, the margins becoming narrower on the feathers of the crown. The bend of the wing is green, as is the carpal edge; only the under-wing coverts are red. The iris is grayish brown.
   Captive status: fairly common. Hahn's Macaw was regularly exported from Guyana during the 1980s.
   Pet potential: excellent. This is the smallest of the macaws, an ideal size for apartments. It breeds readily in aviaries, has a wide range in the wild and occurs in sizable flocks, thus there is no ethical

reason why it should not be kept as a pet.
   Breeding: as easily bred as the more prolific *Aratinga* conures, Hahn's is the perfect avicultural introduction to macaws. These birds do well in suspended or traditional aviaries, usually laying four eggs. The clutch can number between two and five, and the incubation period is 24 days.
   The young spend only eight weeks in the nest. If eggs or young are removed the parents may prove double- or treble-brooded; if the chicks are reared by the parents, they may be only single-brooded. At Bird Paradise, Cornwall, in the United Kingdom, there are two breeding pairs. In one season one pair reared ten young, four in the first nest and *six* in the second. This is the only instance I know of more than five eggs being laid by a small macaw.
   At Loro Parque, Tenerife, there were two pairs. A pair off-exhibit, in an aviary measuring about 3 m

Hahn's is the smallest of the macaws

(10 ft) long, 90 cm (3 ft wide) and 2.1 m (7 ft) high produced four infertile eggs in April 1987. From four eggs laid in the second clutch during the end of May, three chicks had hatched by the very end of June. They were banded on July 17. All three left the nest on August 25.

In 1988 the off-exhibit pair laid the first of four eggs at the beginning of March. The first chick hatched on March 26 and a second chick hatched on March 30. One egg was slightly damaged and so had to be incubated artificially. This hatched on April 2 and was placed in the nest of a pair of Jendaya Conures that had chicks. It was not fed and was therefore returned to the nest of its parents. They killed it. Many macaws and other parrots will accept the pipping eggs of other pairs but will not accept a chick placed in the nest, even when, as in this case, it is their own.

At the beginning of February 1989, I moved from Loro Parque to Palmitos Park, on the neighboring island of Gran Canaria. At that time there were four Hahn's Macaws in an aviary with some *Aratinga* conures. These were sexed and set up for breeding in March, although laparoscopy indicated that one pair was not fully mature. The birds were housed in suspended cages measuring 2 m (6 ft 6 in) long, 1 m (3 ft 3 in) wide and 1 m high.

The more mature pair had four eggs by May 7 (laying dates are not known as I was away at the time). The first egg hatched on May 24, the third on May 28 and the fourth on May 30. The second egg was infertile. The chicks were covered in fairly long white down on hatching. The first and second were banded at 15 days and the third at 13 days with 7.5-mm bands.

Most of the down is lost by the age of seven days but a little remains, mostly on the lower back. At ten days the eyes are starting to slit and are open by 14 days. The beak, which is light on hatching, is now becoming dark, most notably the pads on the upper mandible. At this stage the birds resemble the chicks of small *Ara* species. As they develop and feather, however, to my eyes they look more like the young of the *Aratinga* group which contains the Mitered Conure (*Aratinga mitrata*) and the Red-masked Conure (*Aratinga erythrogenys*), partly because only a small area on the face is unfeathered in *nobilis*.

At Palmitos Park the rearing of the young progressed totally uneventfully. They left the nest on July 18, 20 and 21, that is, after 55, 53 and 52 days. It is also of interest that in the only two breeding pairs of Hahn's with which I am familiar,

Hahn's Macaws aged a few hours and four days, with one egg still to hatch, one that proved infertile and the discarded shell in the background from one that hatched

The same nest (see page 139) ten days later. The chicks are aged fourteen, ten and eight days

the eggs are laid at two-day intervals, whereas in the small *Ara* species which I know, the eggs are laid at intervals of three days, except perhaps by *manilata*.

Another behavioral characteristic which Hahn's Macaw shares with some of the larger *Aratinga* species is that several pairs will live amicably and breed in the same aviary.

Origin: the nominate race, *Diopsittaca nobilis nobilis*, occurs north of the Amazon in eastern Venezuela, Guyana, probably also French Guiana, and northeastern Brazil in Roraima, northern Para, and Amapa.

Natural history: this is a lowland species, preferring semiopen areas. It even occurs on the outskirts of cities, such as Georgetown in Guyana. In coastal Guyana it inhabits sand belts and forest-edged savannas and plantations. Hoppe (1985) observed mixed flocks of Hahn's Macaws and White-eyed Conures (*Aratinga l. leucophthalmus*) which are about the same size and similar in coloration, except for the light-colored beak and a lack of blue on the head. In the field these macaws and conures were distinguishable only by the bare cheek patches and dark beak of the Hahn's.

Nests are usually found in the trunks of living palm trees, at the base of a frond, or in a hollow near the top of a dead palm. Arboreal termitaria are also used.

Conservation: fairly locally distributed but often common, the population of this macaw appears to be stable. Neither trade nor habitat destruction is a threat to it at the present time; thus no special conservation measures are known to be necessary. Guyana is the only

Hahn's Macaw, aged only 36 days but fully feathered. This species develops faster than any other macaw

country which has exported this macaw in any numbers. When a quota system was initiated for the export of macaws from that country in the late 1970s, only Hahn's was exempt as it was stated to be plentiful and well distributed.

Noble Macaw

Plumage: resembles that of the nominate race. The size is slightly larger, about 35 cm (13½ in.).

Weight: about 190 g (6$^{7}/_{10}$ oz).

Beak and eyes: the whitish upper mandible (black in Hahn's) is the most obvious distinguishing feature. The iris is reddish brown.

Immature birds: have the bare skin on the face grayish; there is less blue on the head and no red at the bend of the wing.

Captive status: uncommon because very little trapping for export occurs throughout its range, which is primarily Brazil.

Pet potential: excellent. The same remarks apply as for Hahn's Macaw.

Breeding: biology and behavior do not differ from that of the nominate race.

Origin: south of the Amazon in the interior of Brazil from southeastern Para, southern Maranhao and Piaui south through western Bahia, western Minas Geraïs and Goias to southeastern Mato Grosso and northwestern São Paulo. It formerly occurred in coastal southeastern areas such as Espirito Santo and Rio de Janeiro. Recently it has been found well to the west of its previously known range, in extreme southeastern Peru (Madre de Dios) and northern Bolivia (Beni).

Natural history: the Noble has a preference for open lowland. No significant differences between the behavior of this subspecies and that of the nominate race are known.

Conservation: very little is known about this macaw, or if there are any pressures on its populations.

The Noble Macaw. The color of the upper mandible immediately distinguishes the two subspecies

References

Bertagnolio, P., 1981, 'The Red-tailed Amazon and other uncommon South American parrots', *Avicultural Magazine*, 87 (1): 15

Brockner, A., 1988, 'Zuchterfolg mit Rotbugaras (*Ara severa*)', *Papageien*, 1 (3): 82–3

Delgado, F.D., 1988, 'Save the Panamanian macaws: a project of ICBP-Panama', *Parrotletter*, 1 (1): 12

Estudillo Lopez, J., 1986, 'Psittacines of Mexico: the current situation', 16 pp, unpublished paper, First International Parrot Convention, Tenerife

Fjeldsa, J., N. Krabbe and R.S. Ridgely, 1987, 'Great Green Macaw *Ara ambigua* collected in northwest Ecuador, with taxonomic comments on *Ara militaris*', *Bull Brit Orn Cl*, 107 (1): 28–31

Forshaw, J.M., 1973, *Parrots of the World*, Lansdowne Editions, Melbourne

Gaskin, J.M., 1988, 'Papovavirus infections of caged birds', *14th Annual Vet. Sem. Proc., AFA,* 56–62

Goodfellow, W., 1933, 'Some reminiscences of a collector', *Avicultural Magazine*, fourth series, XI, 414–423

Grummt, W., 1986, 'Breeding rare and endangered birds at the Tierpark Berlin, GDR', *Avicultural Magazine*, 92: 190–195

Harrison, G.J. and L. Harrison, 1986, *Clinical Avian Medicine and Surgery*, W.B. Saunders, Philadelphia

Hoppe, D., 1985, *The World Of Macaws*, TFH, New Jersey

Joshua, S., D. Hunt and J. Parker, 1989, 'Feathers hold the key to a bird's sex', *Cage and Aviary Birds*, March 18: 11

Lanning, D.V., 1982, 'Survey of the Red-fronted Macaw (*Ara rubrogenys*) and Caninde Macaw (*Ara caninde*) in Bolivia, December 1981 to March 1982', unpublished report, ICBP and New York Zoological Society

Low, R., 1972, *The Parrots of South America*, John Gifford, London
1984, *Endangered Parrots*, Blandford Press, London
1986, *Parrots, their Care and Breeding*, 2nd edition, Blandford Press, London
1987, *Hand-rearing Parrots*, Blandford Press, London

Mills, C., 1983, 'Dwarf macaws', *AFA Watchbird*, 10 (3): 22–5

Munn, C., 1988a, 'Macaw biology in Manu National Park, Peru', *Parrotletter* 1 (1), 18–21
1988b, 'The real macaws', *Animal Kingdom*, 91 (5): 20–32

Murphy, J., 1987, 'What you should know about Papovavirus', *Parrotworld*, 5 (2), 52–4
1988, 'Proventriculus dilatation syndrome', *Parrotworld*, 5 (4): 24–6
1989, 'Is your parrot hazardous to your health?', *Parrotworld*, 6 (6): 15–23

Nilsson, G. and D. Mack, 1980, *Macaws: traded to extinction?* WWF/TRAFFIC report

Nores, M. and D. Yzurieta, 1983, 'Distribucion y situacion actual de grandes psitacides en Sudamerica Central', Second Iberian-American meeting of Ornithology, Xalapa, Mexico
1984, *Distribucion y situacion actual de las parabas y parabachis en Bolivia*, ICBP

Pasquier, R. (ed.), 1981, *Conservation of New World Parrots*, ICBP Tech Publ 1, Smithsonian Inst. Press

Porter, S., 1983, 'Notes from South America', *Avicultural Magazine*, fifth series 3 (10): 292

Ridgely, R.S., 1976, *Birds of Panama,* Princeton University Press, New Jersey
1981, The current distribution and status of mainland neotropical parrots , in Pasquier, R. (ed.), 1981
1989, Hyacinth macaws in the wild , *Birds International*, 1 (1): 8–17
Schneider, K., 1985/6, The last feather , *AFA Watchbird*, 12 (6), 8–10
Sick, H. and D. Texeira, 1980, Discovery of the home of the Indigo Macaw in Brazil , *American Birds*, 34 (2): 118–212
Thompson, D., 1986 Avicultural techniques regarding large macaws , First International Parrot Convention, Tenerife, unpublished paper
Volk, S.B. and L.M. Volk, 1983, Captive propagation of Scarlet Macaws , *AFA Watchbird*, 10 (1): 18–23
Westen, H., 1989, Nachzucht eines Rotbugaras , *AZ Nachrichten* (Vereinigung fur Artenschutz, Vogelhaltung und Vogelzucht), 36 (5): 292–4

Picture credits
The publishers would like to express their thanks to the following for kindly providing pictures:

To the author for all photographs (color and black-and-white) with the exception of the following:

Color: Ardea London Ltd/Jack A.Bailey 27 upper; Armin Brockner 83; F.Delgado 127; Ron and Val Moat 23; Dr Charles Munn 27 lower
Black-and-white: Ardea London Ltd/I.R.Beames 8; Armin and Karin Brockner 128 bottom; C.B.Studios 120; Mark A.Clook 47, 48 (both); Ron and Val Moat 97, 102, 132, 134, 138, 141; E.Mussler 14; Parrot Jungle and Gardens, Miami/Busch Gardens, Tampa 88
Drawings: Robin Budden 7; Linda Waters 10

Acknowledgments
The author is indebted to the following who so readily complied with requests for information:

Karin Brockner (W. Germany), Antonio de Dios (Philippines), Dr D. Duffy (Costa Rica), Dr Jon Fjeldsa (Denmark), Dr W. Grummt (East Germany), Barbara Gould (USA), Simon K. Joshua, Olivia Oakes, Robin Pickering, Jerome Scherr (USA) and Phyllis Vahrman, also to R.S. Ridgely, whose paper on the distribution and status of mainland neotropical parrots provided much useful information.

Location of macaws depicted in color
Birdland, Gloucestershire, UK 22; collection of Armin Brockner, West Germany 83 center; Loro Parque, Tenerife 18, 19, 23, 26, 30, 31, 50, 55, 59, 82 upper, 87, 91, 95, 114, 115, 119 upper, 122; Palmitos Park, Gran Canaria 51, 58, 62, 63 upper, 83 upper and lower, 86, 90, 94, 118, 119 lower, 123; Paradise Park, Cornwall, UK 63 lower; Parrot Jungle, Florida 126 upper; collection of Richard Schubot, Florida, 82 lower; Widcombe Bird Gardens, Somerset, UK 126 lower

Index

Illustrations are given in bold type